Creative Ways
to Make Your World
a Better Place

If you've been looking for a way to reinvest your life, to give back some of what you've received, this book is for you. In its pages you'll discover . . .

- ◆ *Practical, workable ideas from women who are creatively giving back in their world*

- ◆ *The right type of ministry for you—and how to get started*

- ◆ *Ways to use your life experiences to help others in similar circumstances*

Whether you've got an extra 15 hours a week or just 15 minutes a day, you can make a difference!

Giving Back

MARITA LITTAUER

Here's Life Publishers

First Printing, July 1991

Published by
HERE'S LIFE PUBLISHERS, INC.
P. O. Box 1576
San Bernardino, CA 92402

Library of Congress Cataloging-in-Publication Data
Littauer, Marita.
    Giving back : creative ways to make your world a better place /
Marita Littauer.
        p.   cm.
    ISBN 0-89840-324-3
    1. Lay ministry. 2. Women—Religious life. 3. Retreats.
I. Title.
BV4400.L57   1991   91-21318
248.8'43—dc20   CIP

Cover design by David Marty Design

Unless indicated otherwise, Scripture quotations are from *The Holy Bible: Revised Standard Version,* © 1952 Thomas Nelson & Sons, New York.
    Scripture quotations designated TLB are from *The Living Bible,* © 1971 by Tyndale House Publishers, Wheaton, Illinois.
    Scripture quotations designated NEV are from *The Good News Bible: Today's English Version,* © 1966, 1971, 1976 by the American Bible Society. Published by Thomas Nelson Publishers, Nashville, Tennessee.

For More Information, Write:
L.I.F.E.—P.O. Box A399, Sydney South 2000, Australia
Campus Crusade for Christ of Canada—Box 300, Vancouver, B.C., V6C 2X3, Canada
Campus Crusade for Christ—Pearl Assurance House, 4 Temple Row, Birmingham, B2 5HG, England
Lay Institute for Evangelism—P.O. Box 8786, Auckland 3, New Zealand
Campus Crusade for Christ—P.O. Box 240, Raffles City Post Office, Singapore 9117
Great Commission Movement of Nigeria—P.O. Box 500, Jos, Plateau State Nigeria, West Africa
Campus Crusade for Christ International—Arrowhead Springs, San Bernardino, CA 92414, U.S.A.

Contents

Introduction

It was ten years ago when my mother, Florence Littauer, felt led to conduct a seminar that has since become known as CLASS: Christian Leaders And Speakers Seminars. That first Speakers Training Seminar which was held in Redlands, California, in January 1981 was going to be a "once only" event. Forty women were invited to attend, hand-picked by my mother and myself. We had met these women in various places across the country as we spoke at different women's groups. Each had been through some kind of trauma or had some story to tell, and each had been invited to this seminar to learn how to tell her story effectively. Thirty-eight of those women came to that seminar, and their stories have since made an amazing impact on their families, churches and communities.

To lead this seminar my mother drew on her background as an English, speech and drama teacher and combined that with her years of experience on the platform, both as a speaker and as an observer of other speakers. That first three-day Speakers Training Seminar lasted four days and evenings and my mother did all the teaching. I assisted her by passing out the papers at the appropriate time and organizing the lunch and dinner arrangements each day.

Since my tasks involved minimal time, I was able to listen to each lady's story. I was amazed at the testing and trauma so many of them had been through. I could see that God had done a mighty work in each of their lives and that He was going to use them and their experiences to help many other people.

At that time I had no idea what God had in mind for the seminar. Although I had helped organize the meetings, I couldn't see how I, at 21 years of age, would be used in its future growth, but I grew along with the program. What started as a handful of women, gathered from around the country, women who were hoping to be able to tell their story without tears, has grown to an international ministry and outreach. We soon wanted to broaden the scope from speakers only to including leaders and writers as well. So we looked for a new title. One day I thought of CLASS, for "**C**hristian **L**eaders **A**nd **S**peakers **S**eminar," and my mother loved the idea that we could "say it with CLASS!"

We now conduct up to ten seminars a year across the United States and even have had one in Australia. CLASS is attended by both men and women and has been particularly helpful to pastors. In 1990 we developed a new form of CLASS designed more for the business community.

CLASS has grown, and so has my involvement. I have attended every seminar since its inception except the one held during the week I got married. As I am writing this I am preparing to go to Australia to teach our second CLASS there. My duties have progressed beyond passing out papers. In addition to overseeing all the various staff and functions of the seminar, I give a living demonstration of the Sanguine personality and teach the section on developing your personal ministry. Through my experience as the chairman and founder of the Southern California Women's Retreat and my interaction with hundreds of men and women who have personal ministries, I help others determine how their lives and experiences can be used to glorify God. It is out of that part of my life that *Giving Back* is written.

In ten years of CLASS, working with people to help them develop their talents and use their gifts, and ten years with my own personal ministry, the Southern California Women's Retreat, I have discovered two basic principles.

First, people would like to use their natural gifts and experiences to help others if they only knew how.

Second, many people think that in order for God to use them they must be a part of an organized ministry or church.

Because of the high visibility of international ministries, people sometimes forget they can be effective right where they are. They don't have to give up their jobs and go into full-time ministry for God to use them. They don't have to have an office or a staff to have a ministry. They can be themselves, in their own home, with little free time or money and God can still use them. That is what personal ministry is all about—that is Giving Back.

Jesus had a personal ministry without any church structure to sponsor Him. He didn't own a building or pass out brochures. His only staff was a disparate group of untrained men who had never been to seminar. Yet God the Father used them to change the world.

He can use you right where you are today.

Giving Back is a collection of creative ideas for personal ministry. In it you will read stories of women like yourself and like me. You will read about the ministries God has given them. Some of these ideas are things you can do all by yourself; some are for you and a few friends; others are for you and your church.

As you read you may find the Lord speaking to you and giving you many new ideas. You will need to seek His guidance as to which is the right one for you. You may not feel led to start any of the ministries mentioned here, but I know if you are willing and ready for God to use you to Give Back to your church or community, God can plant an entirely new ministry idea in your heart, something that may spring up from one of these suggestions.

Oswald Chambers says, "Many of us refuse to grow where we are put, consequently we take root nowhere." Many of us are . . .

so busy telling God where we would like to go . . .
we wait with the idea of some great opportunity,
something sensational . . . but we are not ready
for an obscure duty. Readiness means that we
are ready to do the tiniest little thing or the great
big thing; it makes no difference.[1]

I hope that in a few years I will be writing *Giving Back
Again,* and that it will be full of your stories and of new ideas
brought forth through your ministry and that of others like
you. Yours may be a little thing or a great big thing. "It makes
no difference!"

Section I

Objective

*Now there are varieties of gifts,
but the same Spirit;
and there are varieties of service,
but the same Lord;
and there are varieties of working,
but it is the same God
who inspires them all in everyone
(I Corinthians 12:4-6).*

1

What Is "Giving Back"?

Every man shall give as he is able,
according to the blessing of the LORD your God
which he has given you
(Deuteronomy 16:17).

Several years ago, my father asked a question that has stuck with me. It was a simple question aimed to bring to light the truth of the Scripture that says it is more blessed to give than to receive.[1]

We were all sitting around the dinner table on Christmas day. After several hours of gift opening in which we had conquered an exhausting mountain of presents, we were now ready for a hearty Christmas dinner. As the plates were being passed my father asked each of us to share what gift was our favorite to give. Not which one we liked receiving but which one we were most excited about giving. Without having much time to think, each of us told which gift we couldn't wait to have someone open. We shared the story of why that gift was so special and how we found it. Even the children in the family had made or purchased some special item for Mom or Dad that they knew the recipient was going to love. While Christmas is a wonderful time of receiving gifts, that Christmas was also a special time of giving.

Giving isn't limited to Christmas. Next time you attend a birthday party, watch the gift givers. At a child's party the children will hold their gift up and give it to the guest of honor saying, "Open mine first! Open mine first!" As adults we have become better mannered and have learned to control our excitement about the gift we have purchased. But that joy of giving is still evident. You can tell whose gift is being opened by looking around the room. The giver has stopped talking to others and is leaning in to be sure to see his or her gift being opened.

Giving is a part of our nature and Deuteronomy 16:17 says we are commanded to give according to God's blessing in our lives. Some of our blessings may be financial and our gifts of cash or items of high value are one way that we can Give Back. But what if we are not financially blessed? We are still commanded to give as we are able.

There are many ways to give that are not rooted in money. We can give of our time or our talent. Ephesians 4:8 and 12 tell us: "He gave gifts to men . . . for the equipment of the saints for the work of ministry, for building up the body of Christ."

Each of us as Christians have been given gifts to share with our family, our community and our church. They are to build up the body of Christ. Churches are looking for people who are willing to Give Back. The need is great and the time is now.

The April 14, 1991, issue of *Parade* magazine's article, "Ministers Under Stress," points out the need when it says, "A lot of ministers want congregations to care more about the issues on their doorstep—to become less simply recipients of what the church has to offer and more engaged in providing it to others." If you care about the "issues on your doorstep," you can get involved.

Hebrews 13:16 encourages us: "Do not neglect to do good and to share what you have, for such sacrifices are pleasing to God." Each of us has an opportunity to share our lives with others. Giving Back isn't reserved just for those who have been "called to the ministry." In his classic work, *My Utmost for His Highest,* Oswald Chambers says, "The call of God is not for a special few; it is for everyone."[2]

Giving Back is for everyone. Giving Back doesn't require a special anointing, nor do we have to have obvious abilities; we just need to be willing and available for the Lord to use us.

In our seminars I have heard many men and women say, "I'm not really sure why I'm here. I just feel I need to be ready." Of those who get ready, of those who are available, I have never seen God allow their efforts to be wasted. Many non-traditional and unique ministries have been born as a result of someone being ready and willing.

Recently I got a cute little birth announcement. At first glance it looked like any other. It was pink, indicating a girl, and it listed the "proud parents" and the brothers and sister. As I studied the announcement, I realized it was an adoption announcement for two little girls, Elizabeth Dawn who was 5 years old and Emily Ann who was 4. These were the newest adoptions of the Magnusen family.

I had met Debbie Magnusen while I was speaking at a writers conference and she came to CLASS to learn to

spread the passion and need for her ministry more effectively. It all started when she saw a news story in the late '80s
about a baby who was found in a trash can in Los Angeles—it
had been "thrown away." When Debbie watched that news-
cast, the Lord touched her heart. She called the agency who
had charge of that little life and offered to care for the child.
It was a drug baby, born addicted. While there are long waits
to adopt healthy babies, no one wants these "high risk"
babies.

When Debbie told me her story, I didn't even know what
she meant by the term "high risk" babies. I learned there are
many babies who are born to mothers who can't even take
care of themselves, let alone a child. These babies are left
to become wards of the state.

Debbie and David Magnusen heard about this, and that
was when God touched them and they now take many of
these babies in. The babies are drug-addicted and damaged,
but while they are in the Magnusen's home Debbie loves
them. Some of them eventually go back to their mothers;
others are placed in homes of Debbie's friends. Sometimes,
through Debbie's arrangements, they are even adopted into
those homes, or into her own!

On her own Debbie has done a great deal to give many
a baby a life. She literally has saved them from the trash,
and she has loved them back to life and to physical, emotional and spiritual health!

Debbie didn't start out to have a ministry, but she was
willing to be used by God. Today she does a great deal of
speaking in the Los Angeles area, creating awareness of the
need for families to care for these "high risk" babies. Her
willing heart has saved hundreds of lives.

What about you? Do you sometimes feel God couldn't
use you? If we desire to obey, God will lead the way, and He

will give us the strength we need for whatever task He has placed in our hearts. We see in 1 Peter 4:10,11:

> As each has received a gift, employ it for one another, as good stewards of God's varied grace: whoever speaks, as one who utters oracles of God; whoever renders service, as one who renders it by the strength which God supplies; in order that in everything God may be glorified through Jesus Christ.

God has given us many gifts and He has commanded us to use them, to share them with others and to build up the body of Christ. That's what *Giving Back* is all about!

2

What's In It for Me?

He who sows sparingly
will also reap sparingly,
and he who sows bountifully
will also reap bountifully.
Each one must do as he has made up his mind,
not reluctantly or under compulsion,
for God loves a cheerful giver
(2 Corinthians 9:6,7).

In an era of "looking out for number one," the idea of Giving Back seems opposite to the world's advice to us. God's plan seldom goes along with the current trends or the mood of mankind but His plan is always the right way to go. Years of narcissism have made society see that taking all and giving nothing back has left us personally empty and has stripped the earth of its natural resources.

An article in *USA Today,* in November of 1989, declared the '80s as the decade of narcissism and predicted the '90s would be the decade of altruism. We have looked out for "number one"; we have bought ourselves all kinds of toys; we live in the "right" places and drive the "right" kinds of cars and yet people are as unhappy as ever—and even unhappier! *Fortune* magazine featured an article in its January 29, 1990, issue titled "What Consumers Want in the 1990s." In this article they state:

> Underlying all the changes in consumers' concerns and as important as all of them, will be a markedly changed inner sense. The nineties will see "the end of the myth of me." Narcissism is out, and so is the dog-eat-dog ambition.

The article closes by saying, "Yes, we will still care what things cost. But we will seek to value only those things—family, community, earth, faith—that endure."

Giving Back is something that "endures." It constitutes a value that is important in our lives no matter how busy we may get. We can Give Back in many different ways: It can be as a volunteer through an organized group, or it could be through a simple chat with a friend or neighbor who is having a tough time. What we choose to do isn't as important as the fact that we choose to Give Back.

We often think of giving as being connected with finances, and if our finances are tight, we don't give much. But limiting our thinking to financial giving cuts us out of some of the blessings God has for us. It is like a circle. God gives us gifts; we give them back to Him through serving, sharing and sacrificing for others; and then God blesses us again! In 2 Corinthians 9:6 we see that "he who sows bountifully will also reap bountifully."

The wife of a business associate of mine has been going through a really difficult time in dealing with some pains of her past. I talked with him recently and I asked how she was doing. I was intrigued by his response. He said, "The time when she does the best is when she is helping someone else."

We all have difficulties in our lives at times, but we will do better ourselves when we do as God commanded us to do and Give Back to others the blessings He has given us.

So Giving Back is a command to us from God. Obviously it benefits those to whom we are giving, but as it blesses others it also blesses us, it also gives back to the giver.

The Institute for the Advancement of Health in New York City did a study on how helping others helps the helper. The report of this study is found in the October 1988 issue of *Psychology Today*. It says that the benefits of "helping" range from "more self-esteem" and lifted depression to a high that is likened to the high one gets from exercise. More than 50 percent of those surveyed said that helping gave them a "high" and 13 percent said they've had fewer aches and pains since they began helping others.

The article concludes with this thought: "At this early stage of altruism research, all those selfless people seem to have found ways into a wonderful glow." The research shows that the "glow" lasts indefinitely as it returns every time the experience is remembered. An interesting aspect of the research is that it indicates this "glow" or "high" does not come from giving money, "no matter how important the cause." It comes from close personal contact.

We find in 1 Timothy 4:14: "Do not neglect the gift you have." Each of us has been blessed with so many gifts. We need to pass that blessing on to others by Giving Back!

3

What Could
I Do?

*Having gifts that differ
according to the grace given to us,
let us use them
(Romans 12:6).*

I remember the day I realized I didn't really have a ministry. It was at one of our early CLASS seminars. By this time several other women were a part of the teaching team. On the first day of each CLASS the teaching staff lines up before the assembly and one by one we introduce ourselves. I am the last one to introduce myself to the group because I also introduce my mother. I listened to each of the staff introduce themselves and tell about their ministries, and this day I noticed something. Each of these women had been through some type of trauma, ranging from divorce to death of a loved one and from rebellion to rape. Their ministries and the ministries of other friends I knew all were based on their difficulties and recoveries.

As I looked at my life, growing up in a home with parents who loved me, believed in me and supported me in everything I did, I recognized it was a life free from any major traumas. I thought to myself, *I'll never have a ministry.*

As quickly as I thought that, I mentally raised my hand toward God and said, "It's okay God. I don't want to have a ministry!" I didn't want God to think I wanted a ministry so badly that He needed to give me some trauma in my life!

At that point my credibility for being a part of the CLASS staff stemmed mainly from the fact that I was Florence Littauer's daughter. I used to tell those who attended CLASS that while I was the youngest member of the CLASS staff I was the only one who had had twenty-three years of Florence Littauer's private training.

In addition I was a speaker and author myself. I had been doing color analysis for several years and frequently spoke at diet centers, church women's groups, military wives' organizations and social clubs about what colors they should wear. At 23 I had written a book on color, wardrobe and makeup, called *Shades of Beauty.* Both my book and my speaking were excellent sources for clients for my color analysis business, but they were hardly a ministry.

My friends from the CLASS staff would tell me I had a "charmed life," and I would wonder if there were any ministry opportunities for people with charmed lives. When I shared my concerns with my friends at CLASS, they helped me see that what I did at CLASS in helping people organize their speeches and gain confidence through the correct clothing was in fact a ministry. I was Giving Back to others from the gifts I had at that time, an ability to organize and present things in a simple way, and a good eye for color coupled with an innate ability to put wardrobe items together. Working as part of the CLASS staff and doing color analyses really were more than just jobs. They helped other people, and I found that when women were confident about their clothing, they felt better about themselves.

Since that time, as I have been ready and willing, God has used me to Give Back in many other ways, and I am sure in the future He will increase those ministry opportunities even more.

As CLASS has grown I have found there are many like me. They somehow feel guilty about their "nice" lives and don't see how God could use them; yet they want to be available to God. They want to "have a ministry"—but they don't want to go looking for some trauma to take hold of their lives. So many books which deal with trauma topics have been published in recent years that some of the rest of us inadvertently get the idea God can't use us—we haven't overcome any insurmountable odds. I even heard on TV about a couple who were going to start a support group for people who didn't need a support group so they wouldn't feel left out.

Other people have had some kind of traumatic background but are not comfortable sharing their pains at this time. The pain may be too fresh, or perhaps the perpetrator is still a part of their lives. Whatever the reason, these women also want a ministry but they don't want it based on their crisis area.

In my ten years with CLASS I have found still another group of women looking for a ministry. These women have experienced some kind of trauma in their lives and want to focus on using their experiences to help others who are going through the same thing. Since I help teach the section on developing a ministry, many of these women come to me also. They have a story to tell and a desire to help others, but they need to know how to get started.

Each of these groups of women has one thing in common—a desire to be used by God and to be available to Him to make a difference in the lives of others. Those are the only requirements for Giving Back. The April 8, 1991, issue of *Time* magazine featured a cover story on "The Simple Life." That article points out that what matters is "having time for family and friends, rest and recreation, good deeds and spirituality." Those good deeds take on many forms. That article says,

> Americans are reaching out to strengthen their ties beyond the home. Instead of defining themselves mostly by their possessions and work, more Americans in big cities as well as small towns are getting invloved with their communities. [In fact,] about half of all adults volunteered their time to charitable organizations in 1989, a 23 percent increase from two years earlier.

You may have trauma in your life; God can use you. You may not be ready to talk about your traumas; God can still use you. You may have led a "charmed life" like me; still God can use you. You can make a difference by Giving Back!

On the following pages you will find a collection of stories from women like you. They include many different personal ministry ideas, but they are not just fairy tales. Before you read any further, ask God to use these stories to speak to you. Ask Him to make it clear if one of these ministry ideas is the right one for you.

As you read each story, you will see how that opportunity works and what is involved in developing a personal ministry. If a particular story catches your attention, carefully read the balance of the chapter which will give you complete instructions on starting that type of ministry in your area. If you need more help, you can contact the person who developed that way of Giving Back. Her address is included.

Remember, God can use you. Some of the ideas require quite a bit of time. Others will need some money, and a couple will be done best within a church setting—but none of the ideas will require all three. You don't have to have a lot of time or money. You don't have to have a church or staff to support your ideas. The only thing necessary is a desire to Give Back!

Section I I

Opportunities

*If you give, you will get!
Your gift will return to you in full
and overflowing measure, pressed down,
shaken together to make room for more,
and running over.
Whatever measure you use to give—
large or small—will be used to measure
what is given back to you
(Luke 6:38, TLB).*

4

Women's Retreats

4-A: Facilities

Feed the flock of God; care for it willingly,
not grudgingly; not for what you will get out of it,
but because you are eager to serve the Lord. . . .
your reward will be a never-ending share
in his glory and honor
(1 Peter 5:2-4, TLB).

A few years ago a friend asked me, "Marita, of all the things you do, what is your favorite?"

I only had to think for a minute before responding, "The Southern California Women's Retreat."

While I love working with the publishers and authors that I am in daily contact with as a part of my publicity organization, the thing most personally rewarding to me is running the Southern California Women's Retreat. I refer to it as my "baby." The Southern California Women's Retreat is my "personal" ministry. It's what I do to Give Back.

In some ways I was a likely candidate for this type of personal ministry, but, like you may be, I was also an unlikely choice—and the most obvious reason was my age. I was only 21. The second handicap I had was that I never had done it before. Several things were in my favor for this type of Giving Back, and they are all things I can teach you if you should decide this ministry opportunity is for you!

The idea of a women's retreat started in May, 1981. A group of us from Southern California attended an Arizona Women's Retreat. We greatly enjoyed our time there, but we lamented the fact that we had to drive all the way to Arizona to attend. Someone, it might have been me, said we should have something like this in Southern California. We all agreed and someone else suggested I start one. So there, in a hotel room in Arizona, the Southern California Women's Retreat was born.

As my friend and I drove home, we began planning our first retreat. We came up with ideas for themes, speakers and locations. I talked and drove, and Jan took notes. With my Sanguine personality, I had no shortage of ideas, and as a supportive Phlegmatic, Jan agreed with me.

I know this was truly from God because He provided the support team I needed to make that first retreat a reality. My sister can organize anything, and while I was the creativity behind those early retreats, Lauren saw to it that the ideas weren't lost to my disorganization. She dealt with hotels, getting them down to their best deal, and she created a budget and took care of registration. I chose the final theme, selected the speakers and wrote the brochures. We were a team.

That first retreat was held in a hotel and 125 women attended. Despite several setbacks, which caused us to learn many things the hard way, it was a big success. The hotel we chose trained all of their new employees at the front desk and they were hopelessly inept at checking people into their rooms. The line of women was long and slow-moving, giving many of them a negative attitude before the retreat ever started. However, once the first evening's activities began, the ladies were so happy with what was taking place they forgot about the long line. We made it through the first night with no fatalities!

Since our group was smaller than the capacity of the Grand Ballroom, the hotel had rented the rest of the ballroom to a group of scientists. While we were joyfully singing praises to God at the top of our lungs, they were deeply involved in "evoked potentials." Needless to say, they were not praising with us. In fact, they complained to the hotel that we were disturbing them. In an effort to keep our Christian witness intact, we rearranged our printed schedule so that our times of music coincided with their coffee break times.

Despite our fumbles and inexperience, the women were happy at the end and all wanted to return the next year.

The Arizona Women's Retreat had between five and seven hundred women in attendance each year from all over Arizona and from all kinds of churches. I had hoped that the Southern California Women's Retreat would someday be able to match their success, but I had no idea it would also offer me the joy that it does.

As I fit the planning of the California retreat around my already full schedule, I sometimes think, *This is too much work. I don't have time for this any more. I don't think I'll do it again next year.* But when the retreat happens, I see needs met, I see women come to Christ, and I see lives changed. At the end I read the evaluation forms and I know

I'll do it again next year. The Southern California Women's Retreat is worth every ounce of work and effort.

One year Louise came to me at the end of the retreat and told me she had been watching me and could see the joy of the Lord in my face. She said she wanted that same kind of a relationship with Him. She was a Christian, had been attending the retreat for several years, and was growing in her walk with the Lord. Last year she had a big box delivered to my room in the hotel. The card on top thanked me for being an example to her and for starting the retreat so she could attend. She said she had found the kind of joy in the Lord that she was looking for.

Inside the big box were two large ceramic bunnies, a boy and a girl. I have them in my living room and every time I look at them I am reminded of the retreat ministry.

Since our beginning ten years ago, God has continued to bless our efforts in a mighty way, but we have had some serious scares—like the time the bank lost our deposit of several thousand dollars of registration money. They never did find it; we had to contact all the ladies and reconstruct our entire deposit. Fortunately, Marilyn had excellent records so, even though it was a big job, it was all accurate.

Among the changes we have had to make are some in policy and personnel. My sister Lauren gave birth to her third child and discontinued working on the retreat to become a soccer coach for her older boys. My good friend, Marilyn Heavilin, became the co-chairman and together we have seen the attendance grow from that first 125 to more than a thousand.

We don't have to share the ballroom any more, and we have grown to the point where the retreat is now held in two locations on consecutive weekends in two different cities.

Women now come to the retreat from other states and, like me when I attended in Arizona, they hope to go home and start a similar retreat in their community. You could start one too. It could be for the women of your church, or it could be a larger regional event like mine. Some have as few women as 25 and others have as many as 2500.

The smaller ones have a different flavor from the larger ones, but each is a ministry that can meet the needs of women, men, youth, or even couples. While my retreat is just for women, yours could be for whatever group of people the Lord places on your heart.

How to Get Started

There are several things to decide before planning a retreat of your own. The most important are who will be invited and how they will hear about it. You can't just decide that running a retreat would be fun and expect people to appear. You need a "core group" of interested people first. I had my mother's mailing list, and of course she was a speaker at my first event so I knew many of the women on that list would want to attend. That was my core group.

Your base group mailing list will help you get started. It can consist of people who have attended a particular evangelical function at your church, or a Bible study group, or some other source. It may be those who attend your church every Sunday or mothers from your child's Christian school, but wherever you consider getting your list from, I suggest you plan a retreat only if your core group includes at least a hundred people.

At the most you should plan up to a 20-percent re-sponse. So if one hundred women regularly attend your church, you might estimate a retreat with about twenty of those women.

Selecting a Date and Location

Once you have identified your core group, next you need to select a date and a location. Some of the things to consider in choosing a **date** are major holidays, church functions, and any other events in the community in which your core group might be participating.

You will want to keep your retreat away from Christmas time and summer time. The prime "seasons" for retreats are after school starts in the fall but before Thanksgiving, and after mid-February but before school is out. You would know to avoid the big week-end holidays like Easter and Labor Day, but watch out for those little three-day weekends like President's Day and Martin Luther King Day. Since many families go out of town on these weekends, your prospective people would not be as readily available. Also take note of local athletic events. One year my mother spoke in Indiana during the basketball finals—and the whole town had gone to support their team.

In selecting a **location** for your retreat, you have two main options: a hotel, or a retreat or conference center.

Some of the goals of a weekend retreat should be: (1) to offer those who attend a special time away from the hustle of daily life; (2) to give them some opportunities to improve relationships with one another and with God; and (3) to send them back home refreshed and better equipped to face their daily challenges. In order for these objectives to be accomplished, a retreat really should be an overnight event.

Whether a retreat center or a hotel would be the best for your group will depend on your major goals. If you are planning for a small group of people who already are acquainted with each other such as the women of your church, and your goal is to get to know one another better and have a low-key, relaxing weekend, a conference or retreat center might be the better choice. Most of these retreat or conference centers are located in the mountains, or in wooded or country areas that lend themselves to an intimate, quiet weekend. Additionally, a conference center will offer your group a much more economical package.

If you decide this is the best approach and you don't know of any retreat centers in your area, there are a couple of resources you can use. You can check with the headquarters of your denomination to see if they have a facility in your area (many of them do), or you can contact:

Christian Camping International
P. O. Box 646
Wheaton, IL 60189

They produce an annual directory of all the Christian retreat and conference centers in the United States, listing them by state. It includes information on each facility, such as dates they are open, the size group they can house, and their address and phone number. This is an invaluable resource for anyone planning an intimate type of retreat.

We hold our retreat in a hotel for several reasons. One is, many of the women who attend the Southern California Women's Retreat also attend an intimate type retreat with their own church group. Rather than compete with those retreats, ours is designed to be a totally different experience. In most retreat centers people sleep six to eight in a room on bunk beds and they share a bathroom with several other cabins. While a retreat center offers a cozy environment, a hotel can offer a luxury escape. We want the women who attend the Southern California Women's Retreat to feel pampered. Another reason we use a hotel is, we hope the retreat will be an evangelical outreach. We have found that many women who are uncomfortable going to church and are afraid to go to a conference center in the woods are happy to go to a luxury hotel. They feel less threatened there. They know they can escape to the pool or go shopping if they feel pressured. For us, another plus of the hotel environment is that we don't especially like the camping qualities of a retreat center. We like private bathrooms, hot showers and good beds.

A retreat center is more cozy and relaxed and it will cost less; a hotel's environment is more comfortable and luxurious and it costs more. Either place can be equally conducive to a great weekend retreat so you'll need to make your choice in line with your goals for the weekend, your budget and the needs of your registrants.

Working With Hotels

If you are interested in having your retreat at a hotel, remember they are in business to make money. They are not a ministry and unless the hotel manager is a member of your church, you can expect to get charged for every little thing. If you ask for an extra microphone or an overhead projector, you will find a charge on your bill.

There are several areas where hotel costs can be cut if you know about them. First is finding the right location. For a weekend retreat, look for what is known as a "business property." This is a hotel near an industrial park, business center or downtown location. These hotels are usually full of corporate business during the week and are virtually empty during the weekends. Therefore they are more apt to be flexible on costs for your weekend business. Avoid going to a hotel that is in a resort setting as they will charge you top dollar for your weekend business—unless you book your event in the off season such as Palm Springs in August or Lake Michigan in February.

Once you have settled on a location or two, you can negotiate on the meeting room and meal cost. Hotel food is very expensive. Built into the price of the food is the price of rental for the room in which they will serve you. Some hotels will try to charge you both the expensive food price and a room rental fee. If you are serving their minimum number of people (this number will vary from hotel to hotel and is usually at least fifty), there should be no room-rental fee. If your hotel sales person gives you a proposal that includes room rental, just tell him or her that is not in your budget and you need the room-rental fee waived. If he wants your business, he will remove that cost. If you are serving both lunch and dinner in the hotel as part of your event, you should be able to have all your meeting space free of additional charge.

Be sure to handle these negotiations before you sign a contract with the hotel.

When you plan your meals at a hotel, you must budget for the full cost rather than the quoted cost. When you look over the hotel's prepared banquet menus, you will see fixed prices on them. Unless you have worked in this area before, you may see the price of a luncheon meal and think that is the complete price. In most cases the prices quoted are "plus plus." That means, in addition to the price on the menu you need to figure "plus" tax and "plus" gratuity. This may be as much as a 21-percent price increase over the quoted price. Since math is my weakest area, I tell the hotel what I can afford to spend on both lunch and dinner on Saturday and I ask them to suggest what they can prepare within that "all-inclusive" price. "All inclusive" means the price includes everything—no hidden costs. Currently my all-inclusive meal cost for both lunch and dinner on Saturday is $44 per person.

I usually select a salad or sandwich for lunch and a hot luncheon item for the evening meal. The hot luncheon items are smaller portions than the dinner selections and therefore less expensive than the full dinner fare. For my women's group the luncheon-size servings are more than sufficient. I try to avoid choosing chicken for the evening meal because it seems every banquet I go to serves chicken and I like to have something a little different. One year I selected pork roast with an oriental plum sauce. I was surprised that I only got five or six complaints out of seven hundred women.

Be careful when you give the hotel their meal guarantees. Usually you will have to give them a final count for the meals 72 hours in advance. I have seen many groups lose a lot of money because they didn't understand how the hotels work. Almost every hotel will prepare and set for 5 percent over what you quote them so if you have some on-site registrations, you will be covered, but if you have a lot of "no-shows," you will still have to pay for their food if they were included in the final count you gave the hotel.

To avoid getting stung, I suggest you count the paid registrants you have 72 hours in advance, then subtract 5 percent from that number and use that reduced number for your guarantee to the hotel. They will still set and cook for your actual paid number, but if some people can't come at the last minute, you won't be stuck paying for empty places.

Never add to your paid registrations hoping you will have more people show up. If you do have some "walk-ins" they will probably balance out your no-shows. If by chance your numbers are quite a bit higher than your guarantee, don't worry. The hotel usually can serve the additional registrants something; it just may be different from the originally selected menu.

Serving meals should take care of your room rental cost for Saturday, and hotels are generally willing to be flexible on the meeting room costs for Friday evening and Sunday morning if your group will be renting a number of sleeping rooms. That's one reason it is good to encourage all your registrants to stay at the hotel. Another reason is, they will enjoy the weekend experience more if they get away from home.

Most hotels will give you one sleeping room free for every 25 to 50 rooms your group rents. The Southern California Women's Retreat rents just about 250 rooms at the hotel we use. They give us the presidential suite free of charge and all the speaker's rooms get a complimentary upgrade to the "concierge floor." With as many rooms as we fill they are happy to have our business and they give us all of our meeting rooms free of charge. For a smaller group with no track record of success, you may not be able to get quite as good a deal in the beginning, but it never hurts to try. Remember hotels don't offer bonuses; you have to ask for them.

To keep our over-all registration price down, we do several different things in dealing with the hotel. First we keep the hotel registration price separate from the retreat registration. While we encourage our attenders to stay at the hotel, it is not required. So someone who really wants to come but can't afford the entire package can stay at home and drive in each day.

We arrive at our retreat registration price by adding together the cost of lunch and dinner on Saturday, the fees for speakers and music, the price of brochure printing and mailing, and the expense of the registration packets.

Only those who are actually staying in the hotel require breakfast on Saturday and Sunday, so we include the breakfast cost in the hotel room price. I make special arrangements with the hotel for them to set up a lovely complete breakfast buffet in part of the ballroom. The buffet appears free, it keeps the retreat registration price down, and it provides breakfast for those who need it.

Another arrangement we make with the hotel is for the coffee break. A few years ago I was at a high-budget convention where they charged us so much to attend that they could afford many extra touches. For the breaks they not only provided coffee and tea, but also herb teas, fruits and yogurts. The selection was a delightful surprise, especially for someone like me who doesn't drink coffee.

Since the Southern California Women's Retreat was having Stormie Omartian speak on nutrition the following year, I wanted to offer a healthy alternative to the "coffee break." I knew Stormie was going to tell my ladies they should avoid caffeine so women who would usually gulp down a cup or two of coffee would be feeling guilty and want something else. I went to my hotel salesperson and asked for a "cash break." She didn't know what I was talking about. Many events feature these "cash bars" where each individual walks up to a temporary bar set up by the hotel and pays for his or her own drink. That was what I wanted for my coffee break only I wanted extras like fruit, bran and blueberry muffins and orange and other juices in addition to the usual coffee and teas. The hotel thought my request was a little strange but they agreed to do it. When we have this, it's just like a cash bar—the hotel sets up the break items, mans the sales and keeps the money. All we do is announce it.

Because coffee breaks are so expensive in hotels we never had provided coffee for our ladies in previous years, but once we arranged this cash break, we have had refreshments on Saturday and Sunday mornings ever since. The ladies are so happy with the selection of goodies they can get that almost no one complains about having to pay for them. Now, whenever I attend other functions, I wish they had a "cash break" so I could get some good refreshments during the break times.

4-B:
Program Planning

Selecting a Theme

After you have agreed on a date and have secured a location, you'll need to think about a theme. A theme is important because your speaker selection, your brochure design and your decorations (if you choose to have them) will all need to be based on one primary idea. If your retreat is going to be a smaller event, fewer than a hundred in attendance, and you intend to have just one speaker, you may want to select your speaker first and then plan the theme around that speaker's topics. The theme should be something of interest to your core group, something that will meet current needs in their lives.

For the first several years of the Southern California Women's Retreat we used the same general theme: To Be a Woman of God. Since then some of our themes have been, Women of Light, Divine Design, Run and Be Not Weary, Revitalizing Relationships and A Work of Art. That last theme was based on Ephesians 2:10 which says, "We are his workmanship." We are His work of art. The focus was really on self-esteem, but we chose to avoid those words because some Christians take offense at them.

As we'll discuss shortly, we offer workshops each year. We use the workshop attendance as a survey of individual interests. The year before our "Work of Art" theme, the workshop on self-esteem was the most popular, so, since we recognized it as a subject of great general interest to our group, we made it the theme for the next year. We do this often.

In our tenth year we chose to have a special celebration and invite back all the most loved speakers from the previous years. Our theme was "Bringing You the Best . . . So You Can Be Your Best."

You will want to survey the interests of your core group, either formally or informally, before selecting a theme. If one of the above listed themes would fit your retreat, please feel free to use it.

Speaker Selection and Budgeting

Now you are ready to think about speakers and budget. They go hand in hand because your speaker's fees can determine your budget and your budget can determine who you get for a speaker, and whether or not you have more than one speaker.

As a starting place, I suggest you plan on a minimum of one dollar per person per talk for the speaker. As we'll cover in the section on schedule, most retreats have four or five time slots where they want the speaker to speak. If you are expecting a small group of twenty-five ladies and you want your speaker to speak four times, you should plan on a minimum of $100 for the speaker. This will limit you to selecting a speaker who is local so you do not have transportation costs, and it will also usually limit you to a speaker who is not well known.

If you want a speaker who is more popular and who will attract a higher attendance for the retreat, you'll need to plan on more than a dollar per person per talk. If the retreat center is charging you $45 per person for the weekend including meals, and you expect twenty-five women to attend, and the speaker you want has a fee of $500 for the weekend, you'll need to figure on $5 per person per talk, or a total of $20 per person to cover the cost of the speaker. Added to the retreat center charge, that will give you a total cost of $65 per person.

If you want to provide extra refreshments for the group, or if you need to cover the cost of printing brochures or handouts, you'll need to add a few more dollars per person.

At my retreats each speaker speaks once or twice for a general session. One retreat has about 700 women in attendance and the other has about 400. I can afford to pay each speaker about $500-700 per talk per weekend. If I want a speaker who is very well known and will attract a crowd, I need to plan on those types of fees, and I may need to have that speaker speak three times to be able to afford their flat fee for the weekend. With a large enough attendance I can afford several well-known speakers in one weekend.

A word of warning: Don't plan on a large attendance just because you want a well-known speaker. You'll need to plan realistically based on the size of your core group, to keep your event from being a financial disaster.

Finding a Speaker

There are several ways to seek a speaker for your retreat. Since part of my business is to help various groups find one who will be right for their needs, my first suggestion is that you give my office a call. We'll ask you what type of group you have, how many people you expect, how much you have allotted for your speakers, what your dates are, and if you are interested in any special topic or theme. Then we go through our files of speakers trained through CLASS and find several who would be a good match for both your budget and the needs of your group. We will send you a one-page information sheet on each of the speakers with his or her picture on it, biographical information, and a list of available topics. Under the listing of each topic is a short paragraph to give you a feeling of the flavor and content and the time frame for that message.

Once you have narrowed your selection down, you can call us for sample tapes to review and verify the selected speakers' ability. When you have made your final selection, we will confirm the date, and we will send you a contract and black-and-white photos of the speaker for your promotional purposes.

Rather than sound too much like a commercial, I also need to let you know of other options you have in searching for a speaker. One is to check with your denomination's headquarters to see if they offer a list of recommended speakers. Many do offer such a list, although you probably will have to call each speaker yourself to get promotional materials and tapes.

Another way, though time consuming, is to contact a speaker's publisher. Obviously this technique works only if the person you are interested in is a published author. You can check the back of that person's book to see if a ministry address is listed, or you can write a letter of inquiry to the person, using the publisher's address. Write "Please forward" on the front of the envelope. By the time the letter gets to the speaker, several weeks may have gone by, so be sure to allow plenty of time for this type of search. If you use this method, be sure your letter includes your name, address and phone number.

The last and most commonly used way to search for a speaker is to ask around. Ask everyone you know if they have heard any good speakers lately and if they know how to contact them. This search is also usually quite time consuming so, again, allow plenty of time.

In looking for the perfect speaker for your group, I suggest you use all four types of resources and, no matter where you finally select you speaker from, be sure to listen to tapes of his or her speaking prior to making a final commitment.

If your group is small and you need a speaker who will come for a lower fee, plan on starting your search six months before your event. Lesser-known speakers are not booked up as far in advance. If you are looking for a speaker with quite a bit of recognition, you will need to start at least a year in advance, and for the most popular weekends, maybe even two years ahead.

In addition to a speaker's fee and ability, another major area of concern you need to think of in your speaker selection is variety of topic. If your event will have a large number in attendance and, therefore, you will have a large speaker's budget, the need for variety can be met easily through the use of several different speakers. With a smaller group and only one speaker, that speaker will need to be quite versatile to meet your needs for the entire weekend.

Programming Needs

While you can never keep everyone in attendance happy, that should be your aim. Since people come with different ideas of what a retreat will be, you need to plan your programming in such a way that it touches on everyone's needs at one time or another. I have found five general aspects people look for in a retreat experience. These are of equal importance and therefore are not in any particular order.

Bible Teaching

You must have Bible teaching and usage. Since we are talking about a Christian weekend experience, you'll need to make sure your speaker isn't just sharing a testimony or entertaining. Many people will attend who will think the weekend was a failure if they didn't need their Bibles and they didn't underline some verses. So make sure the speaker you select is a good Bible teacher.

Humor

On the other hand, if the entire weekend is straight Bible teaching, some people will think the weekend was too heavy or not enough fun. So you'll need a Bible teacher who also has a good sense of humor. He (or she) doesn't need to be a comedian, but he does need to have a few funny stories that will make people laugh and add a light touch to the weekend.

Practicality

In addition to your speaker being a Bible teacher with a sense of humor, he will need to be practical. For the teaching that takes place to have lasting effect, the speaker needs to give the listeners something they can put into practice right away on Monday morning. They need some one- two- three steps to make their lives better. This practical information may be part of the Bible teaching or it may be part of a different talk.

When I speak at women's retreats I often give a message entitled "Creative Charisma, Bringing Out the Best in Ourselves and Others." This talk is really a Bible study on good relationships, but it also has a lot of funny stories and is very practical. It meets all three needs we've discussed so far.

My friend, speaker and author Emilie Barnes, is known for her ability to make organization fun. She can get you excited about cleaning your drawers and while her organizational messages are biblically based, they do not require that you have a Bible to follow along. They are light and practical, but when Emilie is at a retreat as the only speaker, she also brings some of her additional messages that do have a lot of Bible usage.

Testimony

The fourth thing you need to consider in your program planning is testimony. People want to hear stories of how God has worked in other people's lives. There may be in the audience many non-Christians, or Christians who are hurting, who will make a commitment to Christ or find new hope for their life through the speaker's testimony. A testimony isn't just the story of how that speaker came to Christ, but also of how God can influence and touch another person.

Inspiration

You'll want to send everyone home on an upbeat note, so you will also need to include an inspirational tone. Your speaker should inspire the hearers to go home and put the new concepts they have learned into practice, to improve themselves as people, and to have a new desire for spiritual growth.

These five areas do not all need to be in one speech or even in one speaker, but if you have one speaker for the entire weekend, that person should be able to meet all five needs. When I am the only speaker at a weekend retreat, I start Friday evening with a talk I call "The Personality Puzzle." This is a presentation on knowing yourself and others better through the study of the four basic personalities, and it is a light way to start when people have arrived exhausted from the trip and the hassle of getting away. This session is both fun and practical.

Saturday morning I present my biblical, practical, humorous message on "Creative Charisma." On Sunday morning I usually speak on "Complete Confidence, Knowing That Where You Are Is Where God Wants You." It includes my testimony and a lot of Scripture, and it is very inspirational.

Those three messages cover all five areas of need for the weekend.

Workshops

If your retreat will have more than a hundred people in attendance, you might want to consider having workshops. Each workshop features a more specific topic that may not be of interest to everyone in your group but that will appeal to enough people to make it still worthwhile. At a women's retreat you might try topics on parenting or marriage, on dealing with pains of the past, or on crafts or health issues.

Workshops are typically offered on Saturday afternoon as alternatives to, or in addition to, free time. They should range from an hour to an hour and a half. In planning your workshop topics, think about all the different kinds of people who will attend and make sure there is a workshop for each group. For example, if you offer a workshop on dealing with difficult teenagers, you'll also need something for those who do not have teenagers and those that don't even have children. If you offer a workshop for working women, be sure there is something else for the full-time homemaker. If you have a workshop geared to the new Christian, you'll need something of interest to the more mature one as well.

If you offer workshops you should have at least three to be sure to have a specialized interest session for everyone in attendance, and a maximum of five to keep the choices simple. When possible, the workshops should be located close to the general session area and easy to find.

The workshop leaders are usually people from your own group who have expertise in a particular area. They usually are not paid, but if possible, their retreat registration should be covered out of the retreat's general budget.

I have found it best to avoid having the main speaker teach any workshop. An exception would be if you have several main speakers and are having only those speakers teach the workshops. When local people lead workshops and the main speaker also teaches one, most conferees will attend the main speaker's workshop making the attendance at the others extremely low. This is embarrassing and unfair to both the main speaker and the other workshop leaders.

Shepherds

You will find it helpful for each of the speakers for your retreat and your workshops to have a "shepherd." The shepherd is assigned to take care of the speaker. This is a special opportunity for a person to get to know the speaker in a more personal way, and people are always delighted with the chance to spend that extra time with the speaker. We ask people to volunteer to be a shepherd on the registration form, but if you are having only one speaker, it would be better just to ask someone to be the shepherd.

The shepherd should contact the speaker by phone or by mail to let her know she will be taking care of her and that she is praying specifically for her. If the speaker is from the local area, the shepherd should call the speaker and offer to drive her speaker to the retreat site. If the speaker is flying in, the shepherd would pick her up at the airport and take her to the site. The shepherd may also prepare a basket of fruit or other goodies for the speaker's room.

On location, the shepherd will help the speaker get settled in her room and make sure she knows the exact schedule. A half hour or so before time for the meeting to begin, the shepherd will go to the speaker's room and escort her to the meeting area. Throughout the weekend, the shepherd will be a companion to the speaker and assist with any needs she might have, such as distributing handouts, helping with the speaker's book sales, and making sure there is water up front for the speaker before the program starts. Recently I spoke at a retreat that I wasn't particularly excited about going to. I had just gotten back from a long trip and I wanted to stay home with my husband, but I had made the commitment, so I went.

My shepherd picked me up at my home and drove me to the retreat center. On the way, we stopped and she bought dinner. In my room she had both a fruit basket with plates, napkins and a knife, and a basket of personal goodies. She had found out I love to cook and I collect bunnies. My goodie basket held some great cooking items—and some bunnies! I couldn't believe she had gone to that extra effort to find out my special interests. I still have the goodie basket on my desk! My shepherd made sure I had someone to eat with so I wasn't alone, a situation that often happens to the speaker. On Saturday afternoon, she took me into a little nearby town for some pie and some shopping along with a few others from the group. When I came home, I told Chuck I owed God an apology for my bad attitude about going—my shepherd had made it my best retreat experience ever.

4-C:
Getting Them There

Preparing the Brochure

Once you have the location, date and speakers selected for your retreat you need to work on promoting it, and your brochure will be a major part of that promotion. Keep in mind that we all get too much paperwork across our desks, through our mailboxes and into our lives. To keep your brochure from getting lost in the shuffle, it must be designed attractively and in colors that will catch a person's eye.

Before you begin working on it, start collecting other brochures you receive that you like, whatever the event or product. Look for attractive and catchy color combinations, interesting folding ideas, and graphics with concepts you might be able to use. Your brochure should be professionally typeset, or, with the multitude of personal computers and graphics programs, you may be able to do it yourself or have a friend or someone at your church do it for you. If you are not personally gifted at writing the copy, have someone else do that.

When you describe the speaker or speakers for the weekend, be sure to include what that speaker has to offer that others should come to hear about. I have often seen brochures where the only thing said about the speaker is that she is a wife and mother. So what? So are more than half of those in the audience. Include what makes this wife and mother someone I should take time from my busy life to come and hear. What has God done in her life? Include what books she has written if that is applicable. I suggest you start the description with something to catch the reader's attention, maybe a question. Then tell what "you" are going to learn from this speaker and end with how "your life will be changed after you hear" what this person has to share.

In addition to the speakers' descriptions and brochure design, a couple of other key things are important for your brochure. Include, as a part of your design, a registration form. If your event will be held in a hotel, you will need two forms, one for the retreat and one for the hotel. Be sure they are clearly marked as to which is which, and ask your hotel sales person to assist you in the design of that part so it will include all the information the hotel needs from each person.

The retreat registration form needs to include the registration price, a place for the individual's name, address and phone number, instructions on who to make the check out to, a place to indicate the total amount enclosed, and the address of where the registration needs to be sent. If you are having workshops, it will be helpful to have a place for the attenders to indicate which workshop they will be attending so you can plan your room assignments and the number of handouts needed. If you are having several speakers, ask people to indicate if they are interested in being a shepherd. If you need additional help with the retreat, such as with registration, prayer or hostessing, you can also provide a space for people to check if they are interested.

Be sure the reverse side of the registration form does not carry vital information. When people tear it off and send it you want them to still have the important details such as date, place and time. In one of our earlier years, we had the map to the location on the backside of the registration form.

Some people noticed it and copied it before sending the registration in, but the last week we had many calls from people who didn't know how to get there because they had mailed us the map! They were right—we had lots of maps, and they couldn't find their way.

If you are offering an early registration discount you will also need to indicate that on the form. I suggest you do have at least one early registration discount, and it needs to be large enough to actually get people to register early for the savings.

At our Southern California Women's Retreat we have three prices. There is nothing listed as an "early registration discount," but in effect the prices are: early discount, regular registration, and late registration. See the sample on the next page.

The early discount is valid only if registration is at least three months in advance, and the late price goes into effect thirty days before the event. We offer a ten-dollar discount for early registration and add ten dollars to the regular registration for the late price.

By giving a significant early discount we find that about a third of our attenders register three months in advance. This gives us the money we need for brochure printing, speaker deposits, airfare and any advance payments the hotel might require. The rest of that early money gets put into a high interest account until the date of the retreat.

When we have really needed cash early, like when the printer gave us thirty days to pay for the brochures, we have offered an additional special that has worked well. Our retreat is held in February or March. I write and design the brochures in September and get them printed and mailed by mid-October. To get the early registration discount our attenders must be registered by December first, but if they

HOTEL REGISTRATION

Check the hotel you will be staying at & mail to same
☐ La Jolla Marriott • March 15-17 • 4240 La Jolla Village Dr., La Jolla, CA 92087 • (619) 587-1414
☐ Irvine Marriott • March 22-24 • 1800 Vonkarman Ave., Irvine, CA 92715 • (714) 553-0100
(please print)
NAME #1 _____ PHONE # _____

ADDRESS _____

CITY _____ STATE _____ ZIP _____

NAME #2 _____ #3 _____ #4 _____

WILL ARRIVE ON _____ WILL DEPART ON _____

Cost of your room does include breakfast and tax. The room rate includes 8% tax:
Single: $80.00, Tw/Dbl: $45.24, Triple: $33.42 Quad: $27.52 (per person per night)
Check-in: 4 p.m. (earlier if possible)   Check-out: 12 noon
Circle one: MC VS AX DN CB DS CD Card number _____ Exp. _____

Credit card will be used as a room guarantee.   Amount of check $ _____

Signature _____

RETREAT REGISTRATION

$60 before Dec. 1, 1990   • $70 before March 1, 1991   • $80 after March 1, 1991
Retreat fee includes admission to all sessions, materials, Saturday luncheon and Saturday evening banquet. We
encourage you to stay at the hotel for continuity of fellowship.
Hotel arrangements are separate. A hotel registration form is attached.
I will be attending: ☐ March 15-17, La Jolla Marriott or ☐ March 22-24, Irvine Marriott

Name _____

Address _____ Phone _____

City/State/Zip _____

Checks payable to Southern California Women's Retreat (SCWR)

Total amount enclosed $_____ (Refundable until March 1, 1991)
Please mail retreat fee and form to: **SCWR, 455 Grant, Redlands, CA 92373**
☐ I am encouraging my friends to join me and need _____ more brochures.
☐ I am willing to help with: ☐ Hostessing   ☐ Prayer   ☐ Registration   ☐ Shepherd
I plan to attend the afternoon workshop on:
Fri: ☐ Stand By   ☐ When Your   ☐ Making Ministries ☐ Sing A   ☐ The 15 Minute
Sat: ☐ Your Man ☐ Dreams Die ☐ of Your Miseries   ☐ New Song ☐ Organizer

register by November first, we offer a fifty/fifty deal: They can have the early registration price, but they pay half of it at that point and the other half on the starting day of the retreat. This plan helps them budget better, and it helps us by giving us cash right away. We had a red rubber stamp made that said:

> Pay $30 by November 1
> Pay remaining $30 at the retreat

and we stamped this on the front of the brochure in the address area. That little special brought a wonderful response.

Scheduling

Every year some people complain that there is not enough free time at our retreat, and some people complain that the workshops aren't offered twice so they can attend two different ones. These complaints, combined with the compliments we get on the programming, have caused us to come up with some ideas for the schedule that we feel are unique.

For our own peace of mind, Marilyn and I started going to the hotel on Thursday evening so we could wake up there on Friday morning, have a relaxed breakfast and make sure the rooms were being set up correctly. We discovered that many of our women were arriving around noon on Friday to avoid the heavy Friday night traffic and to enjoy the relaxation of the hotel. Since so many people wanted to attend more than one workshop and so many were arriving at the retreat in the early afternoon, we decided to offer the same workshops on Friday as we did on Saturday afternoon. It was such a success we have done it for several years now. The pre-retreat workshops start at 3:30 and end at 5:00. Then there is a time for the ladies to get some dinner and check into their rooms if they haven't already done so.

During this break time the hotel offers a sandwich bar in much the same fashion as the cash break mentioned earlier. Since there are too many women to get through the coffee shop in the limited time available, the restaurant has pre-made sandwiches, salads, cookies and soft drinks set up in the registration area. The women can purchase a quick meal and take it to their room, to the pool or anywhere else in the hotel area they might choose. In addition to the time savings, the sandwiches are also less expensive than eating in the hotel coffee shop.

Almost two thirds of those registered for the retreat take advantage of the pre-retreat workshops, and they feel they get a bonus by attending an extra session.

Most retreats start after dinner on Friday evening. Letting people have dinner on their own allows for a lower overall registration fee and gives them time to get off work, get their families squared away and get packed up.

We found that, although the conference itself didn't start until 7 P.M., many people arrived quite a bit before that to get settled into their rooms, have some dinner and be assured of a choice seat. At 6:30 women were already in the main meeting room saving seats and just waiting for the program to begin, so we decided to give them something to watch. We added a pre-retreat concert.

I had some friends who were in a singing group and they had been wanting to perform at the retreat, but I didn't have a` spot for them on the program. Since there were complaints of not enough free time, I didn't want to add anything else. But when we offered this little concert as an optional event before the official start of the program, the early arrivers were delighted.

I quickly discovered this pre-retreat concert provided an added bonus: Everyone was in her seat by 7:00 when we were ready to start. Rather than standing in the hallways or at the back of the room talking with friends, people came in and sat down because there was something going on—this enabled us to start the program right on time.

The pre-retreat concert became so popular that we have extended it from half an hour to an hour. Each year it provides someone new with an opportunity to share his or her talents. When it starts at 6 there are only a handful of people listening, but when they begin hearing the music, those people seem to migrate in, and by 7 the room is full.

Registration

It is best to complete as much of the registration procedure as possible before the day of the retreat: registrant information and collection of money. When the day of the retreat arrives, we have found it helps to have one registration line marked for those who owe money and two or three lines available for the others, according to the first letter of the registrants' last names. It eliminates waiting in several lines if the people working at registration also can hand out name tags and registration packets (see next page).

During the registration period, which for us is the four months prior to the retreat, Marilyn records each check in a notebook noting the check number, the amount of the check, and the names of all people covered with that check. Marilyn marks the amount paid and the check number also on each registration form. If someone else pays for a registration, that is noted on the form as well.

Fortunately, Marilyn's husband Glen is a computer expert and has written a special program on which we can record all the information asked for on the registration form. This can be printed out just before the retreat so our information is completely up to date. If you would like to obtain more information on the computer program, please call the CLASS office and we will put you in contact with Glen.

Your check-in time at the retreat should start at least one hour prior to the first event. So if your pre-retreat workshops start at 3:30, check-in would start at least by 2:30.

Registration Packets

Regardless of what kind of retreat you choose to have, big or small, you will need to give those in attendance a registration packet. It could be a bunch of pages stapled together, a folder full of information, a notebook or a pad.

This packet should include the schedule of the weekend. (Don't give so much information on this schedule that everyone will know if you are a few minutes off.) Give the starting times of each session, what each session is and where it will be held. The registration packet should also contain the printed song sheets if you are using them and any handouts that go along with the speakers' topics.

We like the different aspects of the registration packet to be in different colors so they can be referred to easily during the sessions. Our schedule is always on green paper and the song sheets are on pink. The speakers' handouts are on yellow, salmon, lavender or goldenrod.

If you are having a quiet time assignment, that should be included in the packet also. You might want to include a few sheets of plain white paper or notebook paper for taking notes, and you should include an evaluation form. Ours is always blue. (We will look at evaluations more closely in section 4-D.)

4-D:
The Retreat
Experience

Opening Night

Because some people have to drive quite a distance to get to the retreat and they have a lot to do before they can leave for the weekend, many arrive tired. For that reason, I suggest keeping the first evening's program short and sweet. Don't have more than one main speaker on Friday night. I have seen groups try to have two sessions on opening night, but no matter how wonderful the speaker for the second session is, many of the people are just too tired to stay awake through the program.

Including introductions, welcomes, announcements, singing and speaker, the opening session should not last more than two hours. Offer a program that will be fun and entertaining. Not only will that keep people awake, but it will also be more attractive to those in attendance who are not Christians than a hellfire-and-brimstone message. I have seen first-timers, brought to a retreat by a well-meaning friend, get so turned off by a heavy opening session that they never came back for anything but the meals.

If your retreat will feature both several speakers and some workshops, you'll want to introduce all the speakers and workshop leaders early on Friday evening. After the general welcome and necessary announcements, bring all the speakers and workshop leaders up on the platform to introduce themselves and to share for a minute or two each about what they will be covering in their sessions. This helps people decide which workshop they want to attend, and it identifies the speakers so people can interact with them during the breaks. As a speaker myself, I know how awkward a break time can be if the speaker is just waiting his turn and no one approaches him because they don't know him. Early introductions help to break the ice and give the people who are present something to talk about.

Wrap-Up

After the welcome, announcements, introductions, some music (which we will discuss next) and the main speaker, you will want to wrap up the opening session with prayer and then some final announcements that will lead the group into a time of fellowship. At the Southern California Women's Retreat we suggest the ladies join one another in the coffee shop for pie and coffee or that they head down to the pool area for a late-night swim or a dip in the jacuzzi. We are always amazed as we check out the late-night activity. Little clusters of women are laughing together in the lobby; the coffee shop is full, and the jacuzzi has a constant turnover from the time our meeting gets out until it closes. Since our evening activities are not officially finished until 9 or 9:30, I write into the contract with the hotel that they must keep the jacuzzi open until midnight. Check the closing time of the hotel coffee shop, too. If it closes before your sessions get out or within an hour of your proposed ending, you may want to write a later closing time for that into your contract.

Smaller retreats held in retreat or conference centers often have goodies in a "fireside room" or some similar place that offers a comfortable environment for fellowship. As part of the list of "things to bring" the women are often asked to include a snack to share, and the women munch on these all weekend. If your retreat is the more intimate style, you might want to include some type of mixer to get those who came alone involved in the activities. The close of the first night's program is a good time to give instructions for the mixer as well as announce the fellowship time and location.

Mixers

You can use any type of mixer you choose—I'd like to share with you the best one I've seen. Each person has a name tag made from a 3 x 5 card that was hung around her neck on a string or piece of yarn. Each was instructed to write the initials of her favorite leisure time activity below her name on the card. For example, my favorite leisure activity is sailing to Catalina Island. So, under my name I wrote STCI. People had until after dinner on Saturday to try to guess everyone's activity. All weekend long people were interacting with other people they may not have known previously, trying to guess what the initials stood for. It was somewhat like charades. Someone would ask me, "S—skiing, swimming, sailing?" When she hit one right I would say yes, that was a correct guess, but she still had three letters to figure out. When she finally got them all correct, I wrote my personal initials on her name tag and every time I guessed someone else's leisure activity, that person wrote her initials on my card. By Saturday evening the initials were counted and the person with the most correct guesses, indicated by the most initials on her name tag, won a prize, either a copy of one of the books being discussed that weekend or a basket of bath products.

By doing any kind of mixer throughout the weekend, people continue getting acquainted with one another and finding others with mutual interests. You will hear people saying things like, "Oh, you sail, too? I love to sail."

If the group is small enough, you may want to have them each stand and tell the group what their initials stood for. A variation on this theme could be to have each person write down the initials of their favorite food or vacation spot.

Whether you choose to use my suggestion or any other, you will find a mixer to be a useful activity in any smaller group where people don't know everyone or where some may have come alone.

Music

I am the kind of person who sort of tries to get to church late so I miss the music and arrive just in time for the "real" church. I have virtually no musical talent and I'm happy with an AM radio in my car, but I have learned the value of music as part of the overall retreat plan. I suggest three different types of music: performance, group singing, and praise and worship. All three have a valid place in a program, and they all have specific purposes.

Performance Music

Performance music is a great way to get started. Our pre-retreat concert, a vocal performance by an individual or musical group, gets people's toes tapping and prepares them to be a part of the session's music. We also usually start each morning off with a brief solo, and then the song leader asks every one to join in.

Praise and Worship

While most people know what performance music is, they often question me on the difference between praise and worship and group singing. Praise and worship is the more low-key, reverent style of singing that often involves lifting your hands to the Lord and closing your eyes in prayer. It is moving and contemplative. Many of the songs sung during praise and worship time are direct quotes from Scripture put to music.

Because some people attending the retreat may not be comfortable with this charismatic style of praise and worship, we offer it from 8:30 to 9 on Saturday and Sunday mornings. By separating it from the program, you allow those who want that type of expression to attend and take part, and those who come from a more traditional background can choose to attend just the general sessions. It helps to keep everyone happy by having the worship time before the general sessions.

While this style of singing is meaningful and an important part of the weekend experience, it is often difficult for the speaker to start immediately following praise and worship music. It tends to get the assembly relaxed and reverent and set the stage only for a very serious speaker. If the speaker wants to begin with humor she is fighting a losing battle to pick the people back up and get the audience with her. So we move to something more lively.

Group Singing

Group singing consists of the faster-paced familiar choruses that get the people clapping and tapping their toes. Note that it is more important for the song leader to have an enthusiastic personality than an operatic voice.

We scatter group singing throughout the general sessions as a way to gather the people back to their seats after a break and to give the audience an opportunity to stand up and stretch and get their wiggles out just before the speaker starts.

On the following page are some sample sections of one of the minute-by-minute schedules from the Southern

SOUTHERN CALIFORNIA WOMEN'S RETREAT
1991
Minute-by-Minute Schedule

FRIDAY (MARCH 15 & 22)

1:30	Staff Meeting - Vice Presidential Suite (check with front desk for exact meeting location) Staff meeting for all speakers and support staff
3:00 - 6:30	Registration - Registration booth
3:30 - 5:00	Workshops - Exact location to be announced

SATURDAY MARCH 16 & 23

7:00 - 7:30	Aerobics
7:30 - 8:30	Breakfast Buffet
8:30 - 9:00	Praise & Worship - The Downings
9:00 - 9:05	Connie - opening and welcome
9:05 - 9:15	Group singing Annie & Margie
9:20 - 9:25	Marilyn - registration announcements
9:25 - 9:30	Connie intro Emilie
9:30 - 10:25	Emilie - Things Happen When Women Care
10:25 - 10:30	Connie - intro 20 minute break announce items, location, price, book table and tapes
10:30 - 10:50	Break

SUNDAY MARCH 17 & 24

7:00 - 7:30	Aerobics
7:30 - 8:30	Breakfast Buffet
8:30 - 9:00	Praise & Worship - The Downings
9:00 - 9:05	Connie - opening and welcome
9:05 - 9:20	Group singing

California Women's Retreat so you can see how these various musical options are presented.

Provide the Words

Regardless of whether you choose to have group singing, or praise and worship, or both, be sure to plan on some way for every person to have the words to the music. If hymnals or song books are available, you can use them, although many of them do not have the more contemporary songs favored at retreats. The more commonly used option is to choose a special selection of songs that will complement the theme and goals for the weekend. Your selection should include some favorite choruses most people know and some songs that are chosen specifically because they highlight the theme. If you are not using song books, you can use an overhead projector to display the words for everyone to see or you can include printed song sheets in your registration packet so everyone will have the words.

As Christians we must do everything legally and ethically, and since the words to the songs you are apt to select are copyrighted, you must get a license to reprint the words or use them on the overhead. If your retreat is being sponsored by your church, the church's license should be sufficient since it covers any church-sponsored event. If you hold your retreat independently, as the Southern California Women's Retreat is, you will need to get a license yourself.

At the time I am writing this, I have not discovered any licensing groups that will give you a one-time usage fee. The licenses are good for one year. However, the group we use said they may be coming up with a lesser fee for a one-time use such as an independent retreat. The source I use for licensing is:

Christian Copyright Licensing, Inc.
6130 N.E. 78th Court, Suite C-11
Portland, OR 97218

They authorize you to reproduce and use a large number of popular choruses when you have paid the licensing fee, approximately $150.

Master of Ceremonies

In our earlier retreats we did not have a specific master of ceremonies. Since I was the chairman, I welcomed everyone, made the announcements, introduced the speaker and tried to do all the connecting that was needed. Since I also had to deal with the hotel and solve any problems (the lunch room set up wrong, the room too hot or too cold, or the microphone not working correctly), I found myself out in the hallway most of the time. When I heard applause indicating that the speaker had finished, I dropped what I was doing and ran in to wrap up that session. I'd say, "Wasn't that wonderful?" and gush on when I really had no idea what the speaker had just said since I wasn't in the room for any of the session. I was always out of breath and off key.

One year my sister suggested that we have someone else be the M.C. I was crushed. It was my event and I liked being up front. But I tried to appear noble and we asked someone else to do it. It was the best decision I ever made. Now I wonder why more groups don't place more importance on the position of the M.C.

The qualities to look for in an M.C. are important. She must be able to have a command of the group without appearing bossy. A number of times I have watched in frustration as a perfectly sweet lady has stood behind the microphone and tried to gain control of the noisy group by repeatedly saying, "Everyone please sit down." With her quiet tone, she is easily ignored.

Then there are those like me who simply holler, "All right, it's time to get started." And with one simple bark, everyone falls into place. I get results but no one much likes me for it. Someone who is too loud is not the right choice, nor is someone who is too soft-spoken. Rather, a person who can balance control and grace is needed. We have tried several different options and finally landed on the winning combination: someone with both command and charm.

In addition to her work behind the mike, the M.C. provides the connection, the balance and the continuity that keeps the program running smoothly and on time. To do this she must have a complete minute-by-minute schedule and know the importance of sticking with it. She either should have read books or listened to tapes by the speakers ahead of time. She also should have the speakers' introductory materials several weeks prior to the retreat. By having the materials ahead and reading up on the speakers and their topics, the M.C. will be able to think through her comments leading to and following each speaker, and she will be able to select appropriate Scriptures if she chooses to add them.

The M.C. will open and close each retreat session, make announcements, introduce the speaker, offer comments to connect one session with the next and usually ask the blessing before each meal. By providing this continuity for the retreat, she becomes the string that holds the pearls together.

Saturday Morning

We like to start the day with some form of exercise for those who want it. Because the attenders will be sitting much of the day, it is good to get them moving early. For the more intimate style of retreat in the countryside, an organized walk might be an appropriate activity. In a hotel setting there is little of great interest to see so, rather than a walk, we offer aerobics from 7 to 7:30, before breakfast. We continually have been amazed at the high percentage of the group who want to get up early for exercise. Try to get someone to lead the group who is experienced and can get them all involved.

Breakfast is served from 7:30 to 8:30 and then we offer the praise and worship music from 8:30 to 9 when the morning program officially starts. As you can see from the sample schedule, we usually feature two sessions on Saturday morning with the "cash break" in the middle. Many smaller, intimate retreats will feature the speaker at one session and then have an organized quiet time for the second hour. When I am the speaker at this type of retreat, I am often asked to provide or help prepare a study guide for each person to use during the quiet time. Giving the individuals an outline to follow increases the number of those who use the quiet time wisely.

Lunch

Many of the smaller retreats I have been a part of leave lunch as a social time. They serve a meal in the eating area, but they have no organized program. For that type of retreat, a casual luncheon works very well.

At the Southern California Women's Retreat, and many other larger regional events, lunch is part of the program. If this is your choice, be sure the speaker and topic selected are appropriate for the setting. Lunch is not the time for your heavy Bible teaching or note taking. Since the tables may not be cleared when the program starts, you won't want the ladies writing in or opening their Bibles among the dirty dishes. An inspiring testimony or a humorous presentation that doesn't require a hand-out would be appropriate.

You may choose to have the afternoon free for people to spend relaxing with one another, or you may decide to fill that time with workshops, as we discussed earlier. If you do offer workshops, be sure also to allow for some free time to give everyone a chance to rest and relax before the evening session.

Evening Session

The Saturday night program has been a constant source of struggle for us. At the larger retreats it is a somewhat formal event and the program takes place in the banquet room. When we started out we had the same kind of programming on Saturday night as during the rest of the retreat, but people seemed too tired for it and they wanted something else. We tried a serious dramatic presentation, a monologue on the life of Paul. While half of the audience loved it, the other half really did not. We have had funny skits, and some thought they weren't serious enough. While we know it is not possible to please everyone, we do try to avoid alienating anyone.

We have found that the program must have some meat to it but it must not be too heavy or too serious. What we have discovered works the best for us is a combination musical and testimony type of program. We invite a gifted musician or singer who also has a dramatic testimony to weave into the musical program. Stormie Omartian did this for us in earlier years. We have also had great success with couples like Ann and Paul Downing and Barb and Toby Waldouski. They have been able to match that delicate balance of entertainment and inspiration.

For a smaller retreat, you can still have the banquet feeling. If you have only one speaker, have her choose an inspirational topic for about thirty minutes and have one of the gifted singers from your church give a mini concert. Or if you want to have a more casual tone, just have your speaker give a short inspirational message and then break into teams for an evening of fun and games. I have had a great time at retreats on Saturday evening playing Pictionary. The main thing to remember for Saturday evening, whether your retreat is big or small, formal or informal, is to keep it short and somewhat light.

Sunday Morning

The basic schedule for Sunday morning is a repeat of Saturday morning except it is your closing session. You may want to include a time for an offering, either for a special missions project, next year's scholarship fund or to get the retreat in the black. If your retreat is smaller and more intimate, you may want to have only one session of speaking and allow plenty of time for sharing. You could ask people to share how God has spoken to them during the weekend, or what has been the most meaningful to them.

Never ask for suggestions on how the retreat could have been done better. Asking for ideas will cause people who had no prior complaints to think up problems. Those who have already thought of ways it could be better next year will seek you out and tell you anyway.

Evaluations

The evaluation form included in the registration packet gives people an opportunity to express their appreciation for the weekend. Since I suggest you never ask for criticism, I recommend you call the evaluation form a "Comment Card" or "Comment Sheet." The main things you will want to know from those who have attended are how they heard about the retreat and what made them decide to come, what they expected from it, how they would describe it to others, and what was the most meaningful part of the retreat for them. Also allow room for additional comments. Those who have suggestions for ways you could improve the event for next year can share them here. The answers to all the questions will help you plan next year's program. If a large majority thought there was too much free time, plan more programming next year. If they liked playing games, be sure to include it next year. When you read the suggestions, remember that people seem to comment only on what they don't like. I assume everyone who didn't comment on a specific thing liked it. For example, if I get ten negative comments about the "cash break" out of a thousand women, I assume that 990 of them liked it and I don't let the negative comments depress me.

At the end of a long weekend when you have put in much effort and energy, it is discouraging to receive anything but positive comments. If you can, wait a week or so to read the comment sheets. By then you will have recovered your strength and the few negatives you may get will be more rationally balanced by the wonderful comments of how God has changed lives through your personal ministry.

If you are looking for a personal ministry, a retreat may be just the thing for you. While all of this may sound overwhelming at first, it is really a simple plan. If you start your planning at least a year ahead, you and a friend or two can easily organize the whole thing without the encumbrance of a large committee. If you prefer to work with committees, just assign a different group to each task. You might have a site selection committee, a speaker selection committee, a brochure committee, a prayer group and so on. As the organizer of the event, you will need to keep tabs on the progress of each group and not just assume they have accomplished their goals.

For me, running the Southern California Women's Retreat is my favorite thing to do. It is my way of Giving Back God's blessings in my life and passing them on to many others. If you would like a sample of one of our brochures and a copy of our minute-by-minute schedule, or if you have any additional questions, please contact me by sending a self-addressed, stamped 5 x 7 or larger envelope with appropriate postage to:

> CLASS
> Retreat Information
> 1645 S. Rancho Santa Fe Road, #102
> San Marcos, CA 92069

5

Nobody's Children

Let the children come to me,
and do not hinder them;
for to such belongs the kingdom of heaven
(Matthew 19:14).

It was a hot and humid day for Vermont's Mud Season. A few patches of snow still splotched the ground, but the temperature was hot enough to require opening windows. It was the end of the day, and while it had been a good day I was tired. Nearly a hundred New Englanders had attended our CLASS. Toward the end of the last day those present were in their small groups, and my job was to poke my head into the rooms from time to time to be sure that everything was going well. All the groups under my supervision were, so I decided to go over to the other building and see how everyone else was.

I pushed the door of the old building and it flew open and nearly hit a small child sitting on the steps behind it. She was crying. I bent down and asked her what was wrong. Her dirt-stained face looked up at me and through the tears she said, "My daddy forgot to pick me up."

We conversed briefly and I learned that she attended the Christian school that meets in that building. School gets out at 3, and at 4:30 Heidi was still sitting on the steps waiting for her father. I assured her that with all the people there at the meeting, someone would see to it she got home. That didn't seem to be of much comfort so I asked her if she knew where she lived. She gave me complete directions and I offered to take her home. Heidi brightened up immediately.

On the ride to Heidi's house I discovered that her family had just moved to town a month earlier. Her mother did housekeeping in a nursing home and her father did maintenance work and had a paper route. She had tried to call her mother but she had already left work and they didn't have a phone at home so she couldn't reach anyone. When we got to her house it was an old apartment next to a gas station. The white paint was peeling off, and Heidi told me, "It doesn't look very nice from the outside but it is nice on the inside."

Her mother's car was out front and the door was open. Heidi jumped out of the car and ran into the house. I waited a few moments but no one came out so I guessed Heidi was fine and I headed back to the church.

Heidi is what Valerie Bell calls "nobody's child." She has both a mom and a dad but they are so busy trying to earn enough to pay the rent and put food on the table that somehow Heidi gets forgotten.

When I got back to the church I talked to the pastor's wife and found out that "it's a sad situation" and even that someone from the church pays the tuition to send Heidi to the school. She is frequently left waiting after the other kids have gone home but her dad usually does remember to come after her.

In her book, *Nobody's Children,* Valerie Bell challenges us to look for the "Heidis" in our lives, the children who may have both parents in the home, or may not have. The children who for one reason or another, aren't getting the love and nurture their little lives need. We can offer them the love and support that will help build their confidence and boost their self-esteem, and may even make an eternal difference in their lives.

Valerie herself was one of those children. She was a preschooler when her family moved from an apartment to a home in the suburbs. In the apartment she had layers of other children to play with but in the new neighborhood everyone seemed to be older. Although Valerie had a good home and parents who cared greatly for her, she felt very alone in this new place. Her dad was busy working to make the payments on the new house and her new baby brother had just been born. Valerie's sister was in school already and her mother seemed preoccupied with the care of the baby. While she missed the attention she used to get as the baby of the family, Valerie did like the fact that this left her free to roam about the neighborhood.

Valerie observed the woman next door. She was old and stooped over, and she walked with a cane. She reminded Valerie of the witch in Hansel and Gretel, so Valerie dubbed her "The Witch." Valerie made up stories about The Witch as she watched her from the safety of the bushes. One day as Valerie roamed the neighborhood, curiosity got the best of her and she headed for The Witch's house. When she climbed the steps to the old victorian home, she saw a sign on the door: "Knock once and come in." So Valerie knocked and went in. There she entered a different world. A world where an old woman lived alone with the memories of a mother who had been killed in her youth and a son who had died while he was still a child. "Grandma Wheaton," as she became known to Valerie, had lots of love to give but no one to give it to. Valerie needed a friend who would invest in her young life and make her feel special. Together they filled a void in each other's life. "Grandma Wheaton" told Valerie about Jesus and His love for her, and she was a regular guest at "Grandma Wheaton's" house until her family moved across town a few years later.

Now both Valerie and her husband are involved in Christian ministry, formally and informally, and she looks back at those times with "Grandma Wheaton" as not only good memories but also a strong foundation for her Christian faith. When Valerie was an unruly little kid roaming the neighborhood, "Grandma Wheaton" was there for her.

Today, Valerie has done the same for the children in her neighborhood. Some of the children who land on her doorstep are like she was, from the right side of town with both parents living in the home but maybe working long hours away from home, leaving the children to fend for themselves. Others are more like Heidi and come from an emotionally fragile home life that offers them little support. Some are from divorced homes where Mom has to provide everything and can't be there for her child.

Whatever the reason, parents who care or parents who don't seem to, Valerie's home has become a haven for many of the neighborhood children. At first she resented their constant presence and their intrusion onto her life. She felt these extra children detracted from the time she had with her own two boys who were 3 and 6 years old. But God had other things in mind for the Bell household. He wanted Valerie to love these children who seemed to have no one to care for them. He wanted her arms to be His arms and to wrap these children in His care.

She discovered His direction through a dream. Valerie and Steve had wanted another child, especially a little sister for the boys. She had been praying for a baby and in a dream God told her to look on her doorstep. In the dream Valerie went to the door expecting to see a baby in a pink basket. There was a little boy, not a girl and not a baby. She knew he wasn't hers because he didn't have the trademark dandelion-colored hair, rather he had dark hair. Still, this boy looked familiar. In her dream she said, "God, he's here all the time."

God said, "Why don't you ask him in?" Valerie rushed to bring him in and was filled with the joy of a new mother. The feeling was so intense it woke Valerie up!

When Valerie shared the dream with her husband he agreed it was an unusual dream and suggested that there might be "something to it."

Within a few minutes the phone rang. It was Jason's mother. The divorce was final and Jason's mother was going back to work. She needed some help and was wondering if Jason could go to the Bell's house before school. Valerie told Jason's mother she'd get back to her. As she hung up the phone she thought, *Jason has dark hair. Is it that dark, Lord?*

The before-school help wasn't needed after all, but Jason did become a regular part of the Bell household. While Valerie saw him as an after-school nuisance, a discipline problem, and a potential bad influence on her kids, Jesus saw something more. He saw past the tough-kid exterior to the frightened and frustrated child lurking beneath the hard shell. He knew Jason was living on emotional left-overs, scraps from the ruins of adult lives. Valerie wasn't sure what

God had in mind but she knew it involved sharing the love she was keeping for a new blonde baby with this dark-haired boy.

Jason was the first, but not the last, of the children who made themselves a part of the Bell household. Valerie soon learned to love the ones the Lord brought to her door. She loves the "raggedly dressed, the uncared and untended, the bossy, pushy, sneaky, grabby, dirty, whining children."

Valerie has learned to provide God's love wherever there is need, neglect or abuse. She is learning to be inclusive instead of exclusive and she prays for these extra children in her life. She worries about them and she hurts for them. Valerie has become protective of these "extras" in her life. "I care deeply for someone else's children, the children brought to me not by birth but of the Lord."

As Valerie has become "Ma" to Jason, Jason has grown into a responsible and "potentially great kid." The Lord has blessed Valerie's efforts and she says, "I know He approves whenever I am meeting the need of a child on His behalf."

Valerie prayed for a daughter of her own and God gave her an extra son in need. But, He also gave her a daughter, a little five-year-old named Molly. She was "opinionated and bossy" and she talked incessantly. Her clever ploys of offering to help with the housework gave her an easy entry. She would come home from school, drop off her things at her empty house and head straight for the Bell household. Molly was a latch-key or self-care kid whose father had moved out and whose mother worked full-time, and Valerie felt a need to help with the spiritual vacuum in which Molly was growing up. Under the tutelage of the entire Bell family, Molly learned Bible stories and Christian choruses, and she even learned to pray.

After many years of participation in Molly's life, Valerie's efforts were rewarded when Molly shared with Valerie her plans for the future. She said, "I have something to tell you. I haven't told anybody yet. This summer when I went to the camp your boys go to, I asked Jesus into my heart. I was so unhappy before this summer. But now I'm not. I'm really happy. I want to be a missionary to Saudi Arabia!"

"Opening your heart to another person's child can be a precarious thing—but if you take your chances, you may make a positive difference in one of these children's lives," says Valerie. "Most of us Christians could have a vital ministry right in our own neighborhoods if we allowed the Lord to tenderize our hearts toward the working mom and her children. Think of the potential for evangelism if Christians could capture this vision!"

What about you? Do you have some love you have been saving that you need to share? Could you allow a little friend in your neighborhood into your life? You don't need money and you don't really need much time. Valerie says she doesn't stop her routines for Molly. Molly comes in and helps. They cook and clean together. Since many of these children are used to being alone, they don't require much. They may "follow you around and talk your ears off," but they can fit into your life easily if you'll let them.

Would you consider the possibility that the Lord has this ministry opportunity for you? Are you willing to open your heart to a child who needs your love and attention?

Getting Started

If you feel this ministry is right for you, you will be richly blessed by watching a child progress from one who may be sad, hurting and lonely to a truly enjoyable person. You will see kids from dysfunctional homes where infidelity and swearing are commonplace but who look forward to going to Sunday school and who will eventually invite Jesus into their hearts. The love you share with these children may even spread into their natural homes and make a difference in their parents' lives as well.

These kids are in your neighborhood right now. No matter what side of the tracks you live on, there are families who are hurting. Where families hurt, children need your help. Even if there is no divorce nor a single parent, there may be children who need extra nurture. Both Mom and Dad may live in the house, and they may have a strong marriage, but if their child comes home to an empty house each day, there will be needs you can help fill if you are willing and available.

Have an Inclusive Mindset

First you need a mindset that looks at family in a different way. Rather than thinking of your family as just those who are of your blood and reside under your roof, Valerie suggests you have an "inclusive" mindset.

Inclusive means thinking of your family in a larger sense and including the children in your neighborhood. Changes this may bring about in your household could be things like setting an extra place at the table, cooking differently to include things they like and foods that will expand easily to feed unexpected visitors. Children are always hungry, and if they are at your home, they'll want to snack on something. Valerie says she buys less expensive snacks and larger quantities than she would if she were feeding just her own two boys.

Don't exclude those who don't live at your exact address—be inclusive, and be willing to make others a part of your home.

Give Them Some Space in Your Home

When you reach out to children who need help, comfort or just some extra love, you in effect become a surrogate parent. You want to create an atmosphere where the children feel they belong and are comfortable. This doesn't mean giving them full run of the entire house, but Valerie suggests that you do set up some place for children where they know they are welcome. They need some space where they belong, both emotionally and physically. Valerie and her husband had such concerns about the children who were constantly at their home that they borrowed money to finish their basement and create a strictly kids' space. Their own children and their friends use the basement as much as, if not more than, the extra kids, but everyone knows it is a place where they are welcome.

I have a little friend who lives next door. She loves to come to my house and visit, but I don't have any children and my house is not geared toward kids at all. Still, even in an adults-only house, she has places—really, things—that she knows are within her welcome zone. I have a special collection of make-up that she knows is hers. It is real make-up, not just kids' stuff. Sometimes she knocks on the door while I am getting dressed to go somewhere. I'll let her know I am going to be home for just a few minutes but she can come in. She comes upstairs with me. I get out her make-up and she stands in the bathroom with me and does hers while I do mine. I let her play in my jewelry; she knows what she can and can't touch.

Sometimes I'll be in the kitchen cooking dinner and she'll come down from my bedroom with her make-up on (all over her face) and wearing several necklaces, and she'll say, "I can't find your 'pincher' earrings." I have pierced ears but she knows I have two pairs of clip-ons that she can wear. At my house her space is my vanity and the make-up and jewelry that I keep there for her to play with. She knows that anything of Chuck's is off limits and she stays out of his office and doesn't touch his cars in the garage.

You will need to set your own limits as to how much of your home is open to the children, but do give them some space. If you have children of your own, you may want to give them an entire room or create a special place for them as the Bell family did. Your limits may be between Valerie's and mine. Set your own limits, but set them a little wider than you think you can. Even in an adults-only home like I have, you can still allow a child into your life and give that child his or her own space.

Get to Know Their Parents

With all of the horror stories that fill the news these days, parents should be concerned about anyone who begins to show an interest in their child. The child's parents may be suspicious about your motives. Valerie encourages the "surrogate parent" to seek out the parents of the kids who congregate at her house. Walk across the street and talk to them when you see them come home from work. Tell them good things about their child and let them know you are happy to keep an eye on their child when he is home alone. Wave at the parents whenever they drive by and chat with them when you see them out doing yard work. This will help to create a bond with them and let them know your motives are pure and they can trust you. Additionally, this will help open up communication on an adult level with them for the future. You never know how God may use you to bring about a transformation in that family.

Be Available

This is not just a ministry opportunity for moms who are home all day. Being available doesn't mean you need to be there to take care of a child day in and day out—we are not talking about setting up a child-care business. Being available means being flexible with whatever time you do have.

Valerie works in a part-time situation with a flexible schedule and her job is near her home. In many of the two-career families in her neighborhood, the mom and dad work forty-five minutes away in the city. Valerie allows them to put her name on the child's records at school in case of an emergency where the child needs to be picked up before the parents could get there. Since she drives her boys to school every day, she allows some of the other children in the neighborhood to pile in and join them, even though they could, and usually do, walk.

She is available after school to help with homework if it's needed, and she is frequently called upon by one of her little friends to help fix her hair in a special way for a big day at school.

Like me, your life may have a totally different pace than Valerie's. You can still be available. I take my little friend on errands with me on weekends or even to the grocery store in the evening. I also work close to home and my little friend's mother and father work forty-five minutes away in the city. My name is on her card at school and they can call me if she gets sick and needs to be picked up. One time her mother got delayed at work and she called me to pick her child up from day care because they would be closing before she could get home.

Another time some other little friends in my neighborhood were home alone in the evening when the power went off. Just as Chuck and I were getting out the candles and flashlights there was a knock at the door and there stood three children ranging in ages from 13 to 7. They couldn't find a flashlight and they were scared. We lit the fire and with candles and flashlights, we sat on the floor and played the game of Life until the lights came back on.

It doesn't have to be a big amount of time. The amount you have will depend on your own lifestyle and schedule, but do make some time available to the child or children that God brings to your doorstep.

Remember, This Is a Ministry

If you are going to open your home, and allow God to bring some children into your life, let Him pick who they will be. Pray that He will bring you the children who need your love the most. When you are ready and willing, Valerie says, God will bring them. They will appear on your doorstep and in your front yard.

Often the children who need you the most are not the most attractive children in the neighborhood. Don't treat this as a popularity contest and welcome only the cute and clean children who match your own kids. The kids God sends to you may be the outsiders, the ones with no friends or the ones who are overweight with few social skills. When you pray for God to bring you someone who needs you, don't wait to feel an attraction to that child. If God keeps putting a particular sad soul on your heart and mind, reach out to that child. Make a special effort to include him or her in the activities that may be taking place at your house. Don't exclude those who don't fit the family picture; you may be missing out on your biggest opportunity for ministry.

When you are alone with the child, give him your attention so he knows you are interested in him. Ask him questions about school, friends and family. Listen and try to keep some of the major players in his life in your mind so when he brings those names up over and over again you will remember who he is talking about. This helps to let him know that you really care about him.

Have Realistic Expectations

When you open you heart and home to the kinds of children who need help, you may find that many of them have serious emotional problems. You'll need to realize that you can't meet every one of their needs, and that they won't change overnight.

If they come from a non-churched home, chances are their language will be different from yours and their manners may be rougher than those of your own children. Don't preach at them or try to change them right away. Let them see the way things are done in your house and simply let Jesus shine through you. Before long their attitudes will begin to change, but remember, it is a process and change comes slowly.

Valerie has a group of about fifteen different kids who come through her door during a given week, but two or three are there almost all the time and she has a special ministry to them. She knows she can't meet all the needs of every child who comes to her, but God has given her a few in which she does have an extra interest.

Valerie warns against trying to convert every child who comes or insisting that they all come to church with you. Evangelism is not her primary goal in being involved in the lives of the children in her neighborhood. Her goal is to be there for them. She lets them absorb her attitudes and beliefs as they become a part of her life. When a child keeps returning to her house over and over again, it shows he is attracted to what is taking place there.

Valerie has seen many of these children come to Christ and most of them choose to join them for church on Sunday morning, but she feels it is a choice they have made themselves because of watching Christ's love in action.

Setting Guidelines

Some people are concerned about the bad influence un-churched children might have on their own children or that the lifestyles of these other families may be seem attractive. Valerie has found quite the opposite to be true. Her boys have gained an appreciation for the loving home in which they've grown up. In many cases these children needed an escape from their homes and Valerie's children didn't want to be there either. Valerie sees her boys as having been inoculated by the different lifestyles rather than influenced by them.

Another concern is language that may be used and unruly behavior of children from homes with different standards. Valerie says that since her home is a place they choose to be, not some place they are forced to go for child care, she simply lets them know that if they wish to stay, they will need to abide by the standards of her home. She lets them know that she is in charge. She doesn't allow gossiping or saying bad things about one another and she encourages them to compliment each other. She keeps her word and expects the children to follow her instructions the first time. If she tells them they must all go home by 8 o'clock, when 8 comes she ushers them out. They learn quickly that she means what she says and Valerie says she doesn't have to argue with them, she says something once and they know she means business.

The rules in your home may be different, but whatever they are, let your little friends know them from the beginning. When my little friend started coming to my house she used to whine and fuss. I let her know that was not acceptable behavior at our house and if she continued to whine, she would have to leave. Since she liked to be at my house, I only had to tell her that once or twice before she stopped the whining altogether. She learned that if she was going to be at my house she had to have a "happy face." One day Chuck was underneath his car fixing something when he heard this little voice calling, "Chuck, Chuck, Chuck." He crawled out from under the car and there was my little friend with a big smile on her face. She said, "I'm happy." She wanted to be invited in and she knew she could come in only if she had a happy face.

Valerie has found little difficulty enforcing the rules she has set out for the children who visit her house. She never spanks them or has to send them to a room to sit by themselves. They want to be there and are willing to follow the guidelines she has set up for them in order to stay.

Look around your neighborhood, next door, across the street. Is there a child God has placed on your heart? Valerie Bell says, "You can make a significant spiritual contribution by affecting just one child's life."

If you feel called to be a surrogate parent to a child or children in your neighborhood and you need more information or have additional questions, please read Valerie's book on this subject, *Nobody's Children.* It is published by Word Publishers and should be available through your local Christian Bookstore. If you have additional questions or a success story to share, you may contact Valerie by writing to her at the address below. Please include a self-addressed, stamped envelope.

> Valerie Bell
> Chapel of the Air
> P.O. Box 30
> Wheaton, IL 60189

6

Special Friends

Anyone who takes care of a little child like this
is caring for me! And whoever cares for me
is caring for God who sent me.
Your care for others is the measure
of your greatness
(Luke 9:48, TLB).

A few years ago I was listening to some speakers' tapes for the Southern California Women's Retreat. Among them was one by Colleen Weeks. At this point I don't remember what the exact thrust of the tape was, but I do remember how God used that tape to inspire me.

Colleen was suggesting to mothers of young teenage girls that their teens needed an adult friend, younger than the teen's mother but older than the teen. This friend would ideally be a Christian and a good role model for the teen. The message was geared toward mothers, and Colleen pointed out the value of a responsible adult a child could go to when she had troubles or needed advice on issues she was not comfortable talking with her parents about.

I think this is a great idea, and I remember Dolores who lived with my family when I was in fifth and sixth grades. She was that kind of person to me. Dolores lived in our home for only a couple of years, but she was still a part of our family many years after that. I remember the driving lessons she gave me long before I was old enough to drive and the tips she gave me, along with her smiling face, still flash into my mind every time one of them is needed.

Yes, having a third party involved is a great idea, but that was not what God spoke to me about through Colleen's message. I don't have any children, let alone teenagers. What God told me to do was to be that person for some teens.

My good friend Connie has two beautiful girls and at that time the oldest was heading into her teenage years. I have always loved Connie's daughters and her younger son Benjamin and so I decided I would try to be there for Emily and Amanda. Now they are both teenagers, and while I know I could have done more, and I hope to do more for them, they are special in my life. Emily has borrowed some of my fancy dresses for dates or the prom and Amanda wore my mink jacket to a formal recital. I was pleased to be one of only two adults, other than her parents, who were invited to Emily's sixteenth birthday/beach party. On one visit to my home they expressed interest in my *Victoria* magazine so I sent them a gift subscription. In return they sent me this note:

> Marita—*Thank you so much for your thought-*
> *ful gift. Amanda and I will enjoy* Victoria. *I ap-*
> *preciate the way you let us know how much*
> *you care. You are one of our favorite "grown-*
> *ups"!! (Keep up the good work!)*

I wish I had more time available to be there for Emily and Amanda, but even a little is better than nothing. A friendly chat when I call for Connie, a small gift or being there

for an important event all make a difference. In a note to me
Connie said,

> *. . . Mostly I appreciate the love and attention*
> *you give my children. . . . Nothing can ever*
> *repay the thoughtful time and affection you*
> *have shown them. Thanks.*

I asked Colleen where she got the idea to suggest the
value of a friend like this. She told me that when she was in
her pre and early teens she used to babysit a lot for Wendy's
children. When Wendy, a chatty Sanguine, would return
from where she had gone, she and Colleen would sit and
talk for hours. Sometimes it was in the house, around the
kitchen table; other times it was in the car in front of Colleen's
house when Wendy was bringing Colleen back home.

In fact, Colleen says, many times, late at night Wendy's
husband would be worried about where Wendy was since
she had been gone so long. He would call Colleen's house
and wake up her parents. Her mother would come, dressed
in her bathrobe, and knock on the car window and tell
Wendy that her husband wanted her to come home. Wendy
and Colleen had no idea that hours had passed since they
left Wendy's house.

Like my friends Emily and Amanda, Colleen came
from a good home and she had a positive relationship with
her mother, but this extra adult friend offered her another
place to go with her questions about growing up and her
problems at school.

That relationship with Wendy was so valuable to Colleen that when she married David, she decided she would
be a special friend to a teenager. In her fifteen years of
marriage, she has befriended at least fifteen teenagers. Many
of them still keep in touch with her and one even called her
while in Saudi Arabia for Operation Desert Storm.

Colleen has a unique job. She teaches sex education in Christian schools during the day and as a certified childbirth educator, she teaches prepared childbirth classes to the yuppie types in Orange County, California, in the evening. In addition, Colleen spends one day a week at a special school within the public school system, a school for teenage mothers between the ages of 11 and 19.

Because of Colleen's work with the young mothers she has been able to work with girls from extremely dysfunctional homes. She has heard many stories of sexual abuse in their homes that the girls have never told anyone else, and she has been able to direct them to get help. She has gotten an education in the real world and has had the opportunity to lead many of the girls to the Lord. Her working with these troubled teens may provide them with the only positive influence they get.

Like Colleen and my friends, Emily and Amanda, kids from good homes can benefit from this kind of relationship also. Colleen has known Darek and Marlyessa since they were little children and their parents have been friends with Colleen, David and their daughter Sarah. The friendship started when Darek was little and David was teaching Sunday school. Darek was a wiggly one and Colleen would hold him on her lap throughout the class time.

Through church both families became close friends, and as Darek and Marlyessa grew they would ask to spend the night at David and Colleen's and they often joined them on family trips. David and Colleen went to their graduations and while in college Marlyessa has called Colleen a number of times to discuss boy problems. Darek has brought his serious girlfriends by to meet Colleen and get her approval, and while phone calls from the Gulf War were difficult to come by, Darek called Colleen several times.

Colleen says it is rewarding to see their lives grow and change and to know you have been a part of it. She hopes as her daughter Sarah gets older, someone will fill that need for her.

Just a comment in Colleen's tape spoke to me and has made a difference in the lives of two young girls. You could do the same. If each of us touched the lives of just two, think of how much better a place the world could be.

Getting Started

This is a ministry for everyone. All of us can find a little time to be a friend to a teenager. You don't need to be talented or have a lot of money and you don't even need much time. All you need is a desire to give back and an ear for listening.

Colleen suggests starting with prayer. She asks God to show her the teens that He has ready for her. She has never had to go out and try to find them. When she is ready and available, she says they just seem to appear. Start with prayer and then be aware of the teens the Lord brings into your life.

Next she suggests complimenting them, especially on their mind, how smart, mature or creative they appear to be. Start a conversation with the teens the Lord brings into your life; listen to their ideas and find one you think is at least interesting enough to compliment them on.

Recently Colleen was at party with a family she sees once a year. The previous year the teenage daughter had been into the "dark and dismal" look. She had all black clothes, white pancake make-up and heavy silver jewelry. This year she was into the "hippie" look. She had no make-up, ethnic type clothes, and Birkinstock sandals. The girl had been sullen and silent throughout most of the party when Colleen started to talk to her. As a part of her "hippie" outfit she had on a pretty colored indian skirt. Colleen started the conversation by telling her she liked her skirt. The girl laughed and thought Colleen was making fun of her clothes as most adults had done. Colleen assured her that the skirt was really pretty and she thought that it looked especially nice. Colleen even asked where the girl got the skirt so she could get one for herself. The girl brightened up and she and Colleen had an instant rapport because of a compliment. For the rest of the party Colleen and her new friend talked while the other adults watched in amazement.

Once you have made friends with a teenager, Colleen says the most important thing to do is to listen. It takes lots of listening to lots of little things to allow them to know they can trust you. They will tell you all about their friends and school and anything else that is important in their lives, and while it may seem like unimportant information to adults, you will become a true friend when you show you care enough about them to listen. Once they know you will listen to the little things, they will start coming to you for help and advice on their problems and you may save a young life from disaster.

Additionally it is important to be well read on issues they may be facing so that when they do come to you for advice, you have some answers you can give or at least know of some places they can get the help they need.

Colleen has heard many shocking stories as you may when you are a special friend to a teenager. In some cases you will feel a need to tell the parents. Colleen suggests you let the teen know you are going to have to go to their parents and share what they have told you, unless they do it them-selves. If they resist, she offers to go with them to talk to the parents. She advises that you never talk to the parents without your special friend knowing about it or you will betray the confidence you have built.

Being a friend to teenagers is an excellent opportunity to lead them to the Lord. Rather than witnessing to them right off in the beginning of the relationship, Colleen suggests that you be their friend and offer them wise, biblical counsel when it is appropiate. Allow them to see Christ's love through your life and their personal commitment will be a natural progression.

Being involved in a teenager's life is a rewarding experience. The results are so easy to see as they happen right before your eyes. But teenagers can also be very time consuming. They will drop by anytime and may stay for hours once you have a relationship with them. Be careful that their needs do not come before the needs of your own family. Colleen works with many girls who are young mothers or mothers to-be. She makes sure that her daughter knows she is the most important girl in her mommy's life. She doesn't want Sarah to think she will need to get pregnant to get her mother's attention as some teens do.

Do you to have a desire to Give Back? Do you have a heart for teenagers? If you have that, the rest will happen on its own. Be open to the Lord and be available to make a difference in the life of a teenager.

If you would like more information on being a special friend in the life of a teenager, you may contact Colleen Weeks by writing to the address below. Please send a self-addressed, stamped envelope.

Colleen Weeks
P.O. Box 11221
Costa Mesa, CA 92627

7

Jeffie's Boutique

Any of you who welcomes a little child like this
because you are mine,
is welcoming me and caring for me
(Matthew 18:5, TLB).

A few years ago I was helping my mother pack for one of her many trips and I saw her putting clothes into her suitcase I hadn't seen her wear in years. They were good clothes—some were even favorites of mine—but I knew she had newer things that she liked better. I asked why she was packing those old outfits and she said, "They're for Jeffie's Boutique."

That was when I first heard about Jeffie's Boutique. I had met Jeffie Hubbard at one of our CLASSes, and I remembered her as an unusually funny lady, an older woman and a widow, but I didn't know about her unique little ministry, "Jeffie's Boutique." My mother filled me in.

Jeffie's husband had been in the ministry for many years before he died. Through her thirty-seven years as a pastor's wife, Jeffie always had a heart for those of lesser means. Whenever she heard of a need, she did her best to

99

fill it, either herself or through others. She became recognized as one who knew people with genuine needs and people often gave her clothes, food and other items to pass on to those who could use them.

Her ministry began to take shape when she was given some especially nice dresses. They were brand new and still had the price tags. They came from a woman in a nursing home. The dresses had been gifts from her children, and while she appreciated the gift, she knew she would never have a place to wear them. So, she gave them to Jeffie, knowing Jeffie would find someone who needed them.

When she received the dresses Jeffie didn't think she knew anyone who could use them because they were a tiny size. She prayed that the Lord would show her who those dresses were for. He always sent her clothes just when someone had a need, but she didn't have any idea who these could be for.

Within a short time, a missionary came to visit who had been in the mission field for more than thirty years. She asked Jeffie to take her shopping for some appropriate clothes. They went to the mall and the missionary was shocked at the prices of clothing. The last time she had purchased any in America, she could buy a "nice little dress" for five dollars.

They didn't buy a thing at the mall. In the car on the way home Jeffie mentioned that she had a dress put away that might just be right for her. Jeffie told her she was welcome to try it if she wasn't offended at the offer.

Once they were home, Jeffie got out one of the small dresses she had been given. It fit perfectly! Their husbands both were so pleased with how great the dress looked, Jeffie got out the others. They all fit, and the missionary went on her way with an entirely new wardrobe.

As winter neared, Jeffie got a call from her missionary friend. It was much colder where she was now living than it had been in Africa and she needed a winter coat. She asked Jeffie to keep her in mind in case she received one. Jeffie asked her to pray for a coat. Within a short time, someone sent a coat to Jeffie and it was just the right size.

Jeffie had become a matchmaker for clothes that needed to be worn and people who needed clothes. She never sold them and she seldom purchased those she gave away, but people kept giving her things. In addition to this little ministry, Jeffie is a popular speaker at retreats and church conferences. She frequently had so many extra articles of clothing that she began packing them in her car, taking them with her to the retreats, and making them available to those in need.

While she was attending a district conference for the pastors and their wives of her denomination, the Lord spoke to her regarding her ministry. He told her to create a boutique at next year's conference. She could bring all the clothes she gathered up throughout the year and make them available to the young pastors and their wives. She was so excited about the idea, she asked the person in charge if she could make an announcement. She'd been attending for years and was well loved by the group, and without knowing what she might say, they allowed her to make her announcement. She told them that next year there would be a boutique. It would feature women's, men's, and even some children's clothes, and all the clothes would be free of charge! Needless to say they were excited.

From then on, everywhere Jeffie went to speak, she searched the crowd for well dressed women. She told them about her boutique and how it would meet the needs of the pastors and wives in the smaller churches that couldn't afford many new clothes. She asked them to send her clothes they weren't using. Jeffie only wanted nice clothes, clothes that were currently stylish and in good repair, and she specifically looked for women she thought might be able to help with that goal. Before long boxes of clothes started arriving at her home from all over the country.

When the annual conference came around again, Jeffie was ready. She made several trips in her own car to bring all the clothes she had saved and sorted to the retreat site. She got there ahead of the registrants and, with the help of some friends, set up her boutique. The special things she did to make this an exciting event are discussed later in this chapter.

Jeffie knew there was a need when she started the boutique, but she hadn't realized how great it really was. One of the pastors in attendance told her that her boutique was an answer to their prayers. His wife had not had a new dress in two years and they had been praying she would be able to get one. He was in tears as he told Jeffie of their need and of the blessing the boutique had been.

There are many others like that pastor and his wife. They sacrificially give of themselves and their time to small communities with congregations that can barely afford a pastor, so these pastors often do without many things. Jeffie's boutique fills one of their needs.

Jeffie is blessed by giving, and the recipients are blessed by receiving. Jeffie claims 2 Corinthians 9:11 which says, "He will always make you rich enough to be generous at all times, so that many will thank God for your gifts through us" (TEV). God has provided enough for her to be "generous at all times." People often contact Jeffie regarding a special clothing need they have. They pray together, and God answers with the items they need.

God has given Jeffie Hubbard a unique ministry, but it doesn't have to stay unique. You could start a ministry like hers. It doesn't have to be for the pastors and their wives within your church's denomination, but as you pray and ask for the Lord's direction, He may show you that is where He wants you. You may alter the concept to fit your lifestyle and the way you plan to distribute the clothes, but you can use Jeffie's experience to create your own style of boutique.

Getting Started

When I asked Jeffie for some steps on starting this type of ministry, she emphasized the importance of having the right motive. This is not something you choose to do for your personal gain or glory, but rather because you have a heart and a concern for those of lesser means. If, as you read this chapter, you are moved and feel this is something you would like to do, there are a few things you need to determine: Where will you get the clothes? Where will you store them? And how will you distribute them?

Jeffie recommends this be done without any committees. She does it herself with additional help from her friends and her neice only at the actual boutique. Doing this alone makes it a wonderful ministry for someone who prefers to work without the encumbrance of a committee. If you also have a love for fashion, this may be perfect for you.

Where Will You Get the Clothes?

Jeffie has a built-in advantage in this aspect. Since she speaks to different groups on a regular basis, she has the opportunity to reach many different women about supporting this ministry. If you also travel or speak at various locations, you could do exactly the same thing. If you don't have that source, there are other ways to collect clothing for distribution to those in need. Here are some of the ways we thought of.

While Jeffie gets very little of the clothing she distributes from her own church, your home church would be a logical place to start. Ask the pastor to allow you five minutes of the service one morning to share your vision with the congregation and ask their help. If you plan to distribute the clothing through your denomination's district conference, you should approach the other churches in your region about presenting your plan to their congregations.

Whether you are presenting in your own church or another, have a flyer made up explaining the ministry's concept, who it will benefit, what types of clothing you are looking for, and the address to send the clothing to or drop it off. Ask the congregation to take a few extra flyers to pass out to their friends, neighbors and relatives. We have found that many people will give away clothing when they know there is a specific need but will not dump their discards into a box in a parking lot.

Another option might be to write up a little story about what you are doing and get it published in either your denomination's magazine or your local Christian newspaper. As part of your story, be sure to include the same pertinent information you put on your flyer: what the ministry is, who the clothes are for, what kind of clothes are needed and how to contribute. This will expose your ministry to people you would not be able to reach personally.

Even if your story never gets published, you could include it in your Christmas card or just mail it to all your friends in different parts of the country with a cover letter inviting their support.

Keep some of your flyers or stories with you all the time. Whenever you meet new people, let them know about your ministry. If they seem interested, leave some literature with them so they will be able to contact you regarding clothing contributions.

I'm sure you will be able, on your own, to think up additional ways to gather clothing. The above ideas may help inspire your thinking.

Sorting the Stock

Jeffie has found that by specifically requesting clean, current style clothing in good repair, that's what she generally receives. But some people's ideas of what she wants are not the same as hers so she must sort through the collections. If the clothes are simply dirty, they can easily be washed before distributing them. If they just need a snap replaced or other simple mending, that can be done also. If the items are badly worn, stained, missing buttons, out of date or if they have more extreme problems, Jeffie sends them on to other organized charities who are set up to deal with a larger variety of needs.

Once you have picked out the useable clothing you'll need to sort it into men's, women's, and children's divisions, and then according to size. If you do this regularly as you receive the clothing, the task of setting up the boutique won't be as overwhelming. You can have everything organized and in place before the women arrive.

Storing the Donations

After the clothing starts coming in, storage may be your biggest problem. If you have a basement or an empty bedroom, that can make an ideal storage location. A garage is also suitable, although you may need to cover the clothes to protect them. If you live in an apartment or you just don't have room to store the clothes, check with your friends. One of them might be interested in sharing in this ministry with you by storing the clothes. If your church supports your efforts, especially if you plan to distribute the clothes through the district conference, there may be some room there.

As soon as you have a place to store the clothes, you'll need racks on which to hang them. You can purchase clothing racks through catalogues, organization stores such as Containers and Things in Dallas, Texas, and discount stores such as K Mart or Walmart. If you have a handy man around the house, quite suitable racks can be made from plumbing pipe. Whichever type you end up with, the racks should be able to be folded or dismantled so you can also use them at the distribution site.

Distribution

If you hope to develop your ministry as Jeffie has done and distribute the clothing through a pastor's conference, you will need to get approval from the appropriate channels. I can't imagine any group turning down an offer of free clothes for the men and women in attendance, but I have been involved in church work too long to think that every person who presents an idea like this would be received positively. Prior to going to the area-wide leadership, you should get your local pastor's support and ask him to make the correct contacts for you. Share your vision with the church leadership and ask if they would help facilitate it by providing space and promotion at the annual meeting of the pastors and their wives.

Jeffie lives in Texas and she distributes her clothing collections in Louisiana where she and her husband pastored for many years. Check around with the leadership of your denomination—the biggest need for this type of ministry may not be in your immediate area.

If you reach a closed door through that approach, or if you choose to create this ministry apart from your local church or denomination, you will need to find another group of appreciative people. You may already know of one. Rehab centers, shelters for battered women, and children's homes all have needs that you may be able to help meet. Local community centers may welcome your boutique. If your ministry develops without the church support, you will need to plan a set time, about a year away, for the boutique. If you do go through a church or denomination, you obviously should have the date of the annual conference.

The Big Day

You have stocked, sorted and stored the clothing—the next thing is to get the items to the people whose lives will be enhanced by your Giving Back. This brings us to the day of the boutique. Whatever place you are given to distribute the clothes, try to make it as pretty as possible to avoid having a charity basement feeling. Jeffie has a cute poster she has made out of various fabrics to announce the opening and location of the boutique. The poster shows a little girl poised with a big key in her hand ready to open the closed door of "Jeffie's Boutique." The poster is placed first in the registration area and then toward the front of the meeting room once the sessions start.

When the time comes for the boutique opening, the women are excited. Before opening the doors, Jeffie has a special drawing for brand new articles of clothing. They might include a sweater, a robe or even lingerie, and they are all beautifully wrapped. Jeffie has specially selected these, as some of the donated items are brand new with the tags still on them (such as the dresses Jeffie gave her missionary friend). Others are donations Jeffie has specifically solicited from the larger churches in the district. Each one is wrapped and its contents labeled with a small Post-it Note so it can be given to an appropriate person.

To facilitate the drawing, Jeffie has the names of all the pastor's wives in the district, even if they are not in attendance, in a large glass barrel. The ladies must be present to win, and if a name of someone who didn't come is drawn, her friends let her know what she missed. As the names are chosen and the women come forward, Jeffie's niece sizes up each woman, quietly takes the tag off the box and hands her an item that will fit. The excitement over Jeffie's Boutique has increased the attendance at the conferences because no one wants to miss out on the fun!

If your boutique is not being held for a district conference, you could solicit door prizes from the local merchants, possibly even books or bath products. You might have each woman register as she arrives and then put all those names into a hat for the drawing. While having a drawing isn't necessary for the success of the boutique, it does add to the fun of the day and it makes the boutique an *event*. Jeffie even includes a big ribbon-cutting ceremony to add to the festive excitement.

Before the actual opening, you may want to give the women a map with instructions as to where the various types of clothing and accessories are (women's clothing in one spot, men's in another, and children's in still another) and provide some shopping guidelines.

Depending on the stock you have and the number of women in attendance, you may need to limit the number of items that may be taken on the first day, or the first half of the day if your boutique is only one day. After that time you may open the shopping up to include the men and to allow the shoppers to select as many outfits as they can use. Since all the items are available to the shoppers free of charge, allow them to deplete your stock. If there is any clothing left over, Jeffie takes it to a little mission church where they sell it and use the proceeds for their ministry projects.

Remember the boutique provides a service to those who have excess and to those who do not have enough. Do not treat it as a charity event. Jeffie recommends your attitude showing that you love them and want to do something to make their lives better, not that you feel sorry for them. Make the actual day of the boutique a fun event, a party, and that love will show through. You will be Giving Back!

When my mother spoke at that conference, she took many complete outfits, including shoes and accessories from both her closet and my father's. On the second day of the conference when she stood in front of the group to present her message, she got great joy from seeing how wonderful the women looked in her clothes, some even better than she had looked. My father met several men who fit his clothes perfectly, and he has since sent them additional items. As I finish writing this, I am heading upstairs for a long overdue cleaning of my closet. On Monday, I'll be sending a box of good, current clothes to Jeffie.

Even if you don't feel this is a ministry you want to head up yourself, you can help Jeffie with hers by sending her the clothes you no longer need. It might be even better if you checked with Jeffie to see if she knows of anyone in your area who collects clothes for this type of ministry. If we all send Jeffie our clothes, she may end up with more than she has room to store.

Remember, these clothes are for the people who stand up in front every Sunday morning. Jeffie wants them to have nice clothes. If you would like to send a package to Jeffie or if you would like more information regarding starting your own boutique, you may contact Jeffie at the address below. Please send a self-addressed, stamped envelope with your inquiry.

Jeffie Hubbard
3213 West Ave. T
Temple, TX 76504

8

Fashion Share

*If you have a friend who is in need of food
and clothing, and you say to him,
"Well, good-bye and God bless you;
stay warm and eat hearty,"
and then don't give him clothes or food,
what good does that do? . . .
Faith that doesn't show itself by good works
is no faith at all
(James 2:15-17, TLB).*

I first heard about Fashion Share at one of our CLASS-es in Phoenix. I really don't remember who told me about it but I thought it was such a great ministry, it stuck with me. When I got the idea to write *Giving Back*, I knew it had to be included.

All I knew of Fashion Share was an overview. I was told that once a year, Phoenix First Assembly of God Church hosts a day-long extravaganza designed to reach out to women who may be depressed, discouraged or down and out in the Phoenix metropolitan area. The church has a very active bus ministry, and every Saturday and Sunday they pick up children from all parts of town and bring them to church while their parents often stay home. Fashion Share reaches the women—ages 15 and older—with a special day in their honor. Different women in the church serve as hostesses and are matched up with the various women who are to be invited. The woman from the church makes contact with her guest before the big day, introduces herself and offers to pick the guest up to attend the event. When Fashion Share Day arrives, the woman from the church picks up her guest and befriends her for the day. They watch the fashion show, have lunch, attend the ministry time, and then "shop" together.

By this time, the women of the church and their friends have amassed an extensive collection of high quality clothing, some used, some new. They have collected, organized and artfully arranged the clothing, including shoes and accessories, into a wonderful shopping experience. During this day a friendship that lasts throughout the year is often started between the hostess and her guest. Many of the guests feel loved for the first time in their lives, and they begin attending church, and they accept the Lord. It is an exciting way to make a difference in the life of someone else and see the Lord's work manifested.

While the obvious part of the ministry is a fashion show and luncheon, when I talked with the current director, Sue Gaub, I found it goes much beyond that. I was impressed with the ministry as a fashion show. But when I realized the planning, prayer and additional programming that takes place I was in awe of the dynamics involved. They make Fashion Share worth duplicating in every community in the country.

Phoenix First Assembly holds their annual event every October. It was originally started by Sharon Cook in 1987. The Lord gave her a vision to minister to the women of the inner city. Based on Luke 3:11, which tells us that whoever has two shirts must give to the person who has none, Fashion Share was born as a project to reach out to those needy women and it gives the women of the church an opportunity to participate in that ministry. It brings women of all economic groups together in a unique and wonderful way—and it helps the women in the church take their focus off themselves. Most of the time it gives them an opportunity to minister to the influencer of a family, the mother.

One hostess recalls her experience by saying, "By divine plan, God gave me a hostess ticket from a lady many miles away. I came and met the girl the Lord wanted me to help. She gave her life to the Lord and wants to attend Phoenix First Assembly. The whole theme was a ministry to those who have nothing, to those without love, those with wounds and abuse. The ministry purpose was to set them free through Jesus Christ. Praise God!"

Fashion Share is a full-day event which brings women to the church who wouldn't usually attend. It treats them like "Queen for a day" while presenting salvation and ministering to their inner needs as well. After one guest attended she said, "Although today was the first day I ever spoke to my hostess, I immediately felt as though I've known her as a friend before. She took me under her wing and treated me as though I were royalty. I had been at the lowest point in my life, but today I truly felt wealthy and on top of the world."

Several months ahead of the actual event, invitations are prepared and groups of women from the church head out to invite and register the mothers of the children in the bus ministry and the other women they want to contact. A couple of ladies will approach each home, introduce themselves to the woman and explain who they are and why they are there. They encourage her to attend by pointing out that Fashion Share is presented totally free of charge to the guests. This calms her concerns that there might be a hitch. If she is interested in attending, they register her for the day by finding out her age and shoe and dress sizes. They leave the invitation with her and let her know that her hostess will be in touch with her nearer to the time of the actual event.

As the registrations start coming in, other women at the church tabulate how many women will be attending for the food count, and what all their sizes are so they can be sure there will be at least one outfit for each person. The women from the church also register, and they are paired up as a hostess with a guest who may be of similar age or have children who are close in age so there will a sense of camaraderie.

Meanwhile, back at the church, a major clothing collection campaign has been going on. A brief announcement is made during the morning service and flyers are placed in the bulletin to encourage the women of the church to give some of their clothing and to be involved. The church doors are staffed with volunteers who answer questions, offer additional flyers and accept donations. Each Sunday for eight to twelve weeks prior to the event, the donations pour in.

As a part of the whole process, the women of the church are asked to go to their closets and ask God to show them which of their best outfits He wants them to give. When they request in sincerity, God always shows them what they are to contribute. This not only fills the racks for the day of Fashion Share with quality clothing, but it also teaches the women to listen to the Lord. After they have selected their best, the women are encouraged also to clean out their closets, taking anything they aren't wearing or don't need and donate them—clean, in good repair, pressed, and hung.

In addition to the contributions from the church women, donations also come from the community. Friends and neighbors of the church women clean out their closets and send in their items. Stores in the area donate too. A committee visits the major department stores and local shops presenting the ministry and requesting donations. One store received a shipment of 600 identical pairs of shoes. They couldn't use that many of the exact same shoe so they donated them to Fashion Share. Those shoes have been distributed throughout two years at Fashion Share.

By the time the event arrives it is not unusual for there to be more than 3500 clothing items and more than 1200 pairs of shoes to be given away! The committee who organizes the clothing doesn't turn away any donations. If items are given that don't meet Fashion Share standards, those items are passed on to other organizations with different distribution channels.

A couple of weeks before Fashion Share, each hostess visits her guest, either by phone or in person. She lets her guest know she will be picking her up, gets directions and arranges the time. Sometimes the woman has found she cannot attend as she had planned, and this contact before the event allows for more accurate food preparation.

When the day of Fashion Share finally arrives, the hostesses pick up their guests, bring them to the church and stay with them throughout the day. The program starts off with the glitzy, fun part—the fashion show. The best of the clothing that has been contributed is selected for the show and women from the church model the outfits. Some of the specialty items in the show are distributed to the guests through a drawing—eliminating the possibility of the women fighting over those particular outfits. Door prizes, which have been donated by local merchants, are given to the hostesses as a special thank-you for their giving time and possessions.

As an added feature of the show, there is a speaker who weaves her testimony throughout the clothing presentation.

After the fashion show a catered luncheon is served. This provides a time for fellowship and relaxation. During the lunch the guests are treated to some light entertainment. One year the church invited Spanish dancers to perform; another year they asked a light jazz combo. These provide atmosphere that adds to the quality of the entire day.

The cost of the luncheon is covered through ticket sales and cash donations.

After the lovely luncheon, all the women—both hostesses and guests—go back to the sanctuary for a time of ministry. This part of the program starts with fun, up-beat music that gradually moves into a more worshipful style, setting the tone for the focus of the whole day, the ministry. After the music several short testimonies are presented. These touch on subjects that relate to the needs of the guests: drug abuse, acoholism, physical abuse, abortion, depression and lonliness, and each offers the hope and redemption of Jesus Christ.

Following the testimonies is a time for prayer and dedication. In addition to this opportunity for the women to accept the Lord, counselors are available throughout the day to meet with the women on a one-to-one basis. With as many as five hundred guest women in attendance, this is a time of great ministry, including the hostesses themselves being touched by the love of God. One hostess said, "I was paired with a Hopi Indian girl who asked Jesus into her heart! The testimonies and songs were such a blessing to me. I thank the Lord for allowing me to be a part of this ministry!" The ministry reaches both the guests and the hostesses.

While the ministry time is the basic purpose of Fashion Share, the "shopping" is what initially interests the guests and influences them to attend, and this part of the program follows the testimonies and music. The women are given guidelines as to how many items they may take, which will depend on the number in attendance and the number of items donated. Once the instructions have been given, the shopping starts.

The clothes have been arranged throughout the church and each guest is given a map to help her find the section with her size. There are three separate sections:(1) clothes; (2) shoes; and (3) gift items, which might include purses, belts, accessories and cosmetics. The group is divided into three groups, one group going to each section.

After a given amount of time each group rotates so everyone has a chance to shop in each section. Phoenix First Assembly's Fashion Share is quite large, and they don't want all 800+ women to hit the same place at the same time.

The hostesses stay with their guests and help them make selections that will flatter them and be appropriate for their lives. Some guests come with special needs like the one who said, "Today has blessed me greatly. I'm starting a job and I needed some things to help me out. I've thanked God over and over for giving me this opportunity." Each hostess helps her guest select a complete ensemble that will be appropriate for her, and each guest usually takes home two complete outfits, three separate items and many additional gifts or accessories. Every guest also receives her own copy of a modern translation of the Bible.

Fashion Share is a full day of Giving Back. Like all kinds of ministry, it blesses the one giving as much as the one receiving! Jeffie's Boutique is a clothing ministry designed to be done by one person. It is a quiet ministry that Jeffie works on at a steady pace throughout the year. Fashion Share needs lots of committees and the support of the entire church. The bulk of the work is done just twelve weeks before the event and many people put in long hours to make it the success it is. Either could be a wonderful ministry opportunity for you!

The first goal of Phoenix First Assembly Fashion Share is to reach women in the community by meeting some of their clothing needs, introducing them to and encouraging them in the Lord, and establishing friendships with them through fun, food and shopping.

Their second goal is to encourage their own women to reach out to women in need, to go to the inner city and invite those women into their lives. In broadening their horizons, they receive much joy for their efforts.

Third, the women of Phoenix First Assembly hope to share this project with other churches. They feel that Fashion Share can be done for any size group, and that it can work for any church or community simply by making whatever adjustments would be necessary. This is where you and I come in. I have told you about this wonderful ministry opportunity—now you could start it in your own church.

Getting Started

Phoenix First Assembly is a large church with an active bus ministry, but don't feel limited if your church is smaller and without busses. You can still use the idea to create your own form of Fashion Share. Your guests could be found through community service organizations for women in your area. Your smaller Fashion Share will take on its own tone, but big or small, it can be your own special ministry event. Sue gave me these guidelines to help you create it.

Director

As the director you will be overseeing all the various functions needed for a successful Fashion Share. Start by selecting a few people to work closely with you: an assistant director, some advisors to add a spiritual perspective (often this will include the pastor's wife), and someone who can handle the secretarial work.

When you have your leadership committee formed, you're ready to select a date. As with any of the other functions we've discussed in *Giving Back,* you'll need to be sure your date doesn't conflict with major or minor holidays and you'll need to clear it with the church's master calendar.

In most cases, you, as the director, will develop and handle all printed materials, and you will be involved in the development of the entire day, the time frames and the ministry program.

Time Table

The next step is to develop a time table. Working backward from your chosen date, outline when the various tasks should be completed. Some of the key items to include on your time table are church announcements and clothing collection, visiting and inviting guests, and a cut-off date for registration. You will also need to determine the maximum number of guests and hostesses your facility will hold and/or what you will be able to manage successfully.

Committees and Other Workers

As you can tell, Fashion Share is an involved ministry. Most of the work is done before the actual date, and it takes many people working to make the event a success. The tasks would seem overwhelming if they all had to be done by one person, but when you divide them up among a number of different people, the progress goes more quickly and smoothly. The following is a list of the committees involved at First Assembly with a brief description of each committee's responsiblility. Sue suggests recruiting one or two people for each job and allowing them to add the additonal committee members they need.

Intercessory Prayer Committee. This committee may be made up of women whose schedules or lack of mobility doesn't allow them to be involved in a more active way—and it is vital to the success of the event. They pray regularly for the women who will be attending. Since Satan wants to keep those women in bondage, this committee will also pray to bind Satan and to break his power over the women.

Program Committee. The people on this committee plan the program, which may include music, a skit, etc., and they line up those who will be sharing their testimonies.

Donations Committee. Two to five people are needed to solicit financial support of local businesses and donations of clothing from stores. (Note: It's important to be careful that duplicate requests are avoided.)

Guest Organizer. This job requires an organized person. She keeps track of all the registrations as they come in and matches up guests with hostesses.

Hostesses. The hostess chairman signs up the women in the church as hostesses. Each hostess pays fifteen dollars (this figure may need to be adjusted to meet your costs) for her ticket which covers her attendance and lunch as well as that of her guest and helps to cover the other costs of the day. The position of hostess chairman should be filled by someone who is well known within the church, and who is friendly, yet aggressive.

Promotion and Public Relations. Getting exposure for Fashion Share is important for generating donations, both financial and in clothing. The media attention can also encourage women from outside the church to participate by being hostesses. This job involves getting features in the local papers and announcements on local TV and radio.

Collection of Clothes. This job is accomplished primarily on Sunday mornings. The women who work on this committee are responsible for collecting the donations that are brought to the church on Sunday morning and transfering them to the storage areas.

Organization. The organization of all the donations takes place throughout the week. The women come to the church on a weekly basis, hang up the clothing that has not been brought in on hangers, and sort the clothing and shoes by sizes.

Gift Room. The items in the gift room will be distributed by using a point system. An expensive bottle of perfume may be worth more points than a pair of costume earrings, and each guest has a total of 20 points. The gift room committee evaluates and organizes the gift items.

Outside Churches. This job requires one or two women to visit the other churches in the area to invite their participation either by donations or through hostesses and sponsorships. Other churches are also encouraged to pass on any names of women they know who should be invited as guests.

Decorations. Since part of the concept behind Fashion Share is to make each guest feel like a queen, the decorations are an important part of the day. This chairman will coordinate all the decorations such as plants, silk flowers, banners and any other decorations they might create to make the occasion as festive as possible.

Logistics. This chairman should be able to work well with details since she will be responsible for the rental and arrangement of the fashion show ramps, clothing racks, chairs and tables.

Luncheon. This job involves locating the various catering options and determining which will be the best choice for the day and then working with them on food selection, timing and set-up.

Fashion Show. The fashion show should be organized by someone who enjoys fashion and has an innate organizational ability. She will choose which items are put into the show and select women from the church to model them. She is ultimately responsible for the show itself. Usually a theme or title for the show is chosen. Remember, be flexible; a full-fledged show is not a must, but make it fun for your guests.

One-to-One Counseling. The church should make women available to assist the guests with questions regarding salvation and other issues such as drug abuse or depression. These counselors don't have to miss the entire day but they must be willing to be called out of the program by the chairman to spend time with someone in need. The chairman need not have a great deal of expertise in these areas herself, but she does need to be able to enlist and organize other women with counseling ability. If the church cannot provide women who can do this, you may be able to contact a local counseling center and secure volunteers who would be willing to come for that day.

Most of the jobs that make Fashion Share happen require the work of a number of people. Some of the assignments are very labor intensive while others require less effort until the big day. With this variety of needs, there is a place for every woman in the church to get involved.

Presenting a Fashion Share is a big job with big rewards. When you get comments like these from those in attendance, you know the effort has paid off:

"It was the first time I have been out of the house in almost a year. The only ones I have talked to are my children. I don't feel so alone as I did."

"Fashion Share was truly a blessing to me because around this time in 1987, I was in a shelter for abused women with my four children and another on the way. Even though at that time, I had received Jesus Christ as my Lord and Savior, through your obedience and love for Christ, I have come to know Him as Provider and Protector."

"Today was one of the best days I have ever had. I have never been more moved in my life. I needed to find where I belong and today I have."

Yes, it is worth all the effort.

If you feel Fashion Share is the ministry for the women of your church, I suggest you contact Sue Gaub or the current director at the address below and ask for additional information. Please send a self-addressed, stamped envelope with your request.

Fashion Share Director
Phoenix First Assembly of God Church
13613 N. Cave Creek Road
Phoenix, AZ 85022

9

Parent to Parent

We rejoice in our sufferings,
knowing that suffering produces endurance,
and endurance produces character,
and character produces hope
(Romans 5:3,4).

At 17 Pam was a high school beauty queen. She had already won the local title and was heading for the state competition. She was the envy of all the girls at school, and she dated the football star. Pam had everything going for her. Then, just days before the state pageant, Pam found out she was pregnant, and the dreams of the beauty queen were replaced with the goals of motherhood. She and the football star got married—two high school students who had nothing in common but their good looks and popularity.

In the early years of the marriage Pam gave birth to two lovely girls but they were not enough to keep the marriage together. Pam and her husband separated even before their first child was born, and an in-and-out pattern began that lasted throughout the marriage. Pam and the girls suffered verbal, physical and emotional abuse. As a Christian Pam felt divorce was not an option.

After ten years, Pam was sure her husband, the father of her children, was seeing another woman, and ending the marriage seemed inevitable. At 27 years of age, Pam was a single mother with two daughters under 10.

She knew this was not a positive environment for bringing up children and she did everything she could to make their home the best it could possibly be under the circumstances. Pam read every Christian book she could find on raising children. She knew her girls would carry some scars from their home life into their teen years, and she wanted to help them before it was too late. She tried to put into practice each new technique she learned. Some helped; some didn't.

In her search to provide the best home for her daughters, Pam prayed for a husband and a father. Within a short time she met Bill. Although he had never been married, he was sure he would be a good father. Because of his experience as a probation officer Bill had worked with lots of kids in the past.

Bill and Pam were married and at first everything was wonderful. They became one big happy family, like Pam had always wanted. Bill was a good father and he took the girls into his life as if they were his own. Amidst wedded bliss, Stephen was born into the family. Together Bill and Pam continued their parenting education for their new family, through both reading books and attending seminars.

As the girls were heading into adolescence they were strong-willed, and Pam sought the advice of a professional

counselor to help her deal with the difficulties. There were no real crises yet, but Pam wanted to do all she could to help her daughters deal with their low self-image and to try to prevent troublesome teenage years. She saw it as preventative medicine.

In keeping with their preventative parenting mind set, Bill and Pam attended a drug prevention seminar. The girls were now in the adolescence and early teenage years. Bill and Pam attended several workshops at that seminar and one of them seemed to provide some answers to their problems. It was called "Back in Control" and it presented a parenting style similar to what they had grown up with themselves. They changed their approach with their daughters and became much more strict. At the same time they became involved in a movement with the Christian community to ban rock music from their home and especially from the girl's lives.

Bill and Pam were parenting out of fear. They were afraid they were losing control. They were afraid their girls would get into trouble, and they were afraid of the influences of the world on their girls. Bill and Pam were doing everything they could to help the family and make it strong, but it wasn't working.

The world their girls were growing up in was not the same world in which they had grown up, and the parenting styles that had worked for their parents weren't working for them. The "Back in Control" approach may have worked for parents in the fifties, but today's kids were facing different issues and the approach that seemed to make things better at first, in time created more problems. As the girls got older things got worse. They rebelled and were very demanding.

When her older daughter was in the ninth grade, Pam got a phone call to come to the school—her daughter was sick. At first Pam accused her daughter of faking it or tricking her. As her symptoms increased Pam could see something was really wrong. At the hospital Pam discovered that her daughter had taken an overdose of prescription drugs. As a routine procedure, the state investigated the case. While no abuse in the home was found and no fault was placed, they did recommend counseling for her daughter. Her daughter became involved in a therapy program through the hospital and she began to improve in some areas but in others she became worse. Then Pam's younger daughter began to have problems.

Pam and Bill's home life was out of control. In desperation they tried to force the girls to behave and reinstated the "Back in Control" approach. They even went to the training center for this technique and got extra training. Because of his experience as a probation officer, Bill's approach to parenting was through power and the "Back in Control" method made sense to him, but both girls continued to get worse.

Their older daughter was arrested and spent the night in Juvenile Hall. Still searching for answers, Bill and Pam had been through several counselors, a number of books and many parenting approaches. During this time, they stumbled upon a "reality therapist." She suggested they attend a parenting seminar she was teaching. What she said made sense and they signed up. What they learned was very different from any of the other programs they had been exposed to. Throughout the nine weeks of the class they were able to see immediate changes in their home life as they applied the new techniques. Finally they had found some answers.

Before, Bill was trying to parent from a position of power, but now he was winning not by force but through cooperation. The power struggles lessened and there were instant payoffs. While it was awkward at first, the kids could see the changes and responded positively.

Pam was so excited to finally have something that was working for them that she started teaching the program for the women at church. The teaching made the new concepts more a part of her life, and because of that her parenting style was changing faster than Bill's. The women who were in Pam's class were excited about the new concepts they were learning, just as Pam had been. They wanted their husbands to take the parenting class, too, so Pam went home and asked Bill if he would consider them teaching as a team what they had learned. Bill could see Pam's increased growth through teaching the classes, and since they had taken the class together, he understood the value of others taking the training as a couple. Together, Bill and Pam started a couple's parenting class in their home. Many of the women who had been in Pam's class at church came and brought their husbands, some of them sent their friends, and Bill and Pam invited their neighbors. The class went well and a number of families were changed within the nine short weeks.

Teaching together had been a blessing, not only for those in attendance, but for Bill and Pam as well. Just as Pam had found while teaching the class at church, so Bill discovered that he was able to make the techniques and concepts more a part of his everyday life when he had to study them to teach. Pam and Bill grew together, and their parenting skills and their home life continued to improve rapidly.

After that first class that Bill and Pam taught in their home, they had several others there, and then they started teaching at the church. Because of the church's schedule the classes had to be reworked to fit into a shortened time frame. This was the first time Bill and Pam changed their program from the original one that was laid out in the leader's guide. They kept the basic format and added their own stories and examples. When they added their own stories they found people responded even faster because they learned better from real examples than from just the workbook. The classes at the church filled up right away and soon had a long waiting list to get into the class.

Bill and Pam were being personally blessed in many ways because of their Giving Back. First there was the increased understanding of the material and the easier input into their own family system. Bill and Pam also grew closer together as a result of their team teaching. They had the joy of seeing the lives of entire families change right before their eyes. Bill found that many of the basic relational skills they were teaching also carried over into his work and they made him a more effective manager. Bill and Pam plan to keep teaching parenting classes as long as there are people who want to learn. Bill said, "This is the most rewarding thing I have ever done. I have to keep teaching these classes."

With that as a goal, they thought they needed to get some training. Neither of them had had any previous teaching experience; they just had a story and personal examples. Pam came to our CLASS to improve her communication skills so she could become a better teacher. During the intense three-day training Pam gained confidence in her ability and in God's direction for her life. She learned how to better use her personal story throughout the classes she teaches. Then Bill and Pam together took the training offered by the creators of the parenting techniques they had been teaching.

They found they had been doing a good job teaching the S.T.E.P. (Systematic Training for Effective Parenting). The additional training and the certification bolstered their confidence and credibility. Now, they not only had their own story but they also had official training in the subject area. Shortly after that Bill took three days off work and attended CLASS.

At the present time Bill and Pam have been teaching parenting classes for almost four years. They have gone from a one-time small group in their home to several years of classes with a long waiting list at their church. Now they offer their classes through a local counseling center. Their son's elementary school heard about their program and is offering the classes through the P.T.A.

Five years ago their home was in turmoil and their lives were in crisis. They were afraid the girls were too old for any changes. While the road has had a few bumps, the family is in a far healthier place today than it was then. Today their oldest daughter, who no longer lives at home, will drop by just for a visit because she misses Mom and Dad. They are helping their daughters make wiser choices for their own lives and are allowing them to live with the consequences of those choices. Their son is growing up in a home that is very different from that of the girls and his choices are much wiser at a younger age. Both Bill and Pam work in regular jobs and teach their parenting class one or two nights a week. Pam knew all the hard work as a mom had paid off when her oldest daughter recently came to Bill, her stepdad, and Pam, and said, "You guys really love me, don't you?" It is never too late!

What about you? What experiences have you been through in your life that could be used to help others? You could Give Back through a class setting such as Bill and Pam have done. Your experience may be in parenting as theirs is—it may even be through the same parenting material—or it may be something totally different. My friend Emilie Barnes began teaching classes twenty years ago to help women conquer an area she had struggled with and won.

Today she is one of the best known advocates for women's time management and organization skills within the Christian community. Emilie never set out to write books or teach seminars across the country. She just started teaching little classes in her home to help women get organized. What she did helped women and the ministry grew.

When Bill and Pam attended that first S.T.E.P. parenting class, they never expected to be teaching it over and over again. They never thought they would become certified parenting instructors. Like Emilie, they were just open to God's direction in comforting others with the same comfort God had given them (2 Corinthians 1:3,4).

Getting Started

If you have been through some difficulty in life and you feel called to help others who are dealing with the same issues, follow Bill and Pam's example and allow the Lord to use you to Give Back to those in your church or community.

Find Your Area of Expertise

First you need to identify your area of expertise. If you feel called to this area of ministry, you probably already have step one mastered.

Materials

Next you need to decide what material you are going to teach. If your help came through the form of an existing program that has a leader's guide like S.T.E.P., then you'll already have the material available. Although, like Bill and Pam, you may later find you want to personalize the material you present, don't feel you must do that the first time you teach it. There is a saying in the world of professional speaking: "Stick with what brung ya'." That means if you do one thing well or one method has worked for you, stick with it.

If the ideas you wish to teach are not from a book or leader's guide, but rather from your own personal experience, you have a couple of options. You can write your own material or find something that already exists and work with it.

Unless you have done a lot of work with teaching and leading small groups, I suggest you find some material to work with that is similar in nature to your own personal experience. Since you have been through that trauma or difficulty, you will teach it with more passion than someone who merely picks up the leader's guide in a Christian bookstore and decides to teach it. Many people all over the country are certified parenting instructors with S.T.E.P. as Bill and Pam are, but few of them have classes as popular because they don't have the personal experience behind the teaching.

In looking for leader's guides and teaching materials for your subject area, visit the best full-service Christian bookstore in your community and ask someone there to look up available guides on your subject area. Many Christian organizations have publishing arms that produce a great variety of small group guides and although they are not widely distributed outside the organization, they are available to the general public if you know to ask for them.

The Navigators have NavPress, Moody Bible Institute has Moody Publishing, and Campus Crusade for Christ has Here's Life Publishers, and they all have a wonderful selection of small group guides.

Preparation

After you have the material you wish to teach, you will want to study it, make it a part of your life and plan to include some of your own personal examples before you try to present it the first time.

Finding an Audience

When you feel ready to teach, either go to your church's leadership and offer to teach a Sunday school class or women's program in your area of interest, or invite in a group of friends and neighbors to your home for a class. If, like Bill and Pam, the subject area is something that has really changed your life and those in your church and community have seen the transformation in you, they will be anxious to allow you to teach or to attend themselves. Most churches have few strong Christians who are willing to make a leadership or teaching commitment. Assuming there has been a positive change in your life, they will welcome your efforts.

Promotion

Help the church get the word out by giving them the needed information regarding what the class is about, what those who attend will learn and how it can change their lives. Be sure to include the five journalistic *W*s: *Who* is teaching it and who should attend; *What* the class is and what it is about; *When* it will be held and when it will end; *Where* the class is being offered (your home or the church); and *Why* people would want to attend.

If you are teaching the class without the church's involvement, you will need to spread the word about your class in other ways. Make up flyers yourself with the same information on them; pass them out through your neighborhood; post them on community bulletin boards; ask your local Christian bookstore to pass them out to their customers; mail invitations to your friends.

Reservations

Even though there may be no charge for your class other than perhaps the cost of the guide book, ask those who are interested to call and reserve their space. This will allow you to be prepared with enough materials, refreshments and seating. For the best interaction and teaching, Bill and Pam found that a group of about ten to twelve was the ideal size.

Group Guidelines

If the nature of your subject is highly volatile and emotional, like Bill and Pam's, you may want to establish some group guidelines before starting. Bill and Pam have posted them on a large board in the room during each meeting as a reminder. The guidelines they use from S.T.E.P. are:

1. Stay on the topic.
2. Become involved in the discussion.
3. Share the time.
4. Be patient—take one step at a time.
5. Encourage each other.
6. Be responsible for your own behavior.

Your First Class

When your first class starts, you may want to have each person in attendance share who they are and what experiences they have had that brought them to your class. This will help build a good sense of group camaraderie. Assuming the interest is there, continue teaching your class through the designated material, allowing some time for teaching and some time for discussion each week. In Bill and Pam's class, the teaching is 50 percent and the discussion is 50 percent. They give their listeners assignments to be accomplished during the week that will make the material being taught a part of their lives.

Once Bill and Pam had taught their first nine-week class, they knew they had something valuable for both themselves and those in attendance.

Additional Training

After you have taught your first couple of classes, and you find your subject area is something people are interested in, your material is helpful to them, and you enjoy the time you invest in teaching and preparation, you should get some additional training before expanding your class any further. Like it was for Bill and Pam, you may discover that the promoters of the material you are teaching offer an advanced class or some certification you could take to boost your confidence and credibility. Our CLASS (Christian Leaders And Speakers Seminars) would be an excellent next step for you as it will help you personalize and organize your material while building your presentation skills.

Polishing and Perfecting

By the time Bill and Pam began teaching S.T.E.P. at their church, the reworking they did to fit the church's schedule produced an even better class.

When you have taught your class several times and have had some additional training, either through advanced teaching on your subject or through a seminar like CLASS, you should rework your material to polish and perfect it. Be sure to include plenty of your own stories and the success stories of those who attended your previous classes.

Bill and Pam taught their parenting seminar through the church for several years and continually reworked and updated the material they were presenting. Although they still use the original S.T.E.P. program that changed their parenting style five years ago, the classes they teach today are much more polished, and are more a part of their personal lives, than when they were simply going over the exercises in the workbook.

Growing

They have now expanded their ministry beyond the church and into the secular community through their son's school. Before redirecting their teaching energies, Bill and Pam trained another couple to carry the parenting classes at the church.

Take your experiences and use them to help others. Make a difference in your church or community by Giving Back!

If you have any questions or comments about how you can start a parenting or other class in your area, you may contact Bill and Pam through CLASS. Please include a self-addressed, stamped envelope for the reply.

Bill and Pam Lehtonen
c/o CLASS
1645 S. Rancho Santa Fe, #102
San Marcos, CA 92069

10

Making Ministries From Miseries

The same Good News that came to you
is going out all over the world
and changing lives everywhere,
just as it changed yours
that very first day you heard it and understood
about God's great kindness to sinners
(Colossians 1:6, TLB).

For many of us the thought of having been abused as a child is incomprehensible. The idea of dealing with a divorce is devastating. The reality of rape is repugnant. But for many more, these miseries are facts of life that haunt them daily. The Christian community as a whole has become more in tune with the needs of those who fill its churches on Sunday morning, and a multitude of material has been produced to help the victim become victorious.

As a result, we have seen a new movement, an awakening within the Christian church, called recovery.

Perhaps you, like my friend Yvonne, have been a part of that process in the last few years. And like Yvonne, you may feel God calling you to use your experiences to help others along their path to healing.

Yvonne Martinez is a petite and attractive young woman. She has the kind of face that invites you to tell your story, but the smile and comfortable manner reveal none of the horror she has lived and grown through. The Lord has brought Yvonne a long way to turn her miseries into ministry.

Yvonne grew up in what we call today a dysfunctional family. Her father was in and out of prison and drank heavily when he was home. One night her parents were at the home of some friends. While the adults played cards, the friend's son entertained Yvonne by playing house. As a 4-year-old, playing house was a favorite activity of hers, but this teenage boy's version of "house" was different from what she and her little friends played. The room was dark, her panties were off and he molested her.

A few years later, Yvonne's father came home drunk and attacked her mother. Yvonne heard her mother's cries for help and tried to rescue her from her father's grasp. Yvonne was pushed away. Somehow she and her family eventually reached the safety of her grandmother's house. A divorce trial was to follow and Yvonne's father, angered by Yvonne's agreement to testify against him, said, "You turned against me so I am disowning you. I don't ever want to see you again." As an 8-year-old, Yvonne didn't know how to react but she knew she must be a very bad person for her father to say those things.

Still looking for the love she never received, Yvonne married at 18. The life of parties, drinking and motorcycles didn't fill the void. After two years, Yvonne was pregnant and she was sure that this child would give her the love she'd longed for. While Yvonne saw the child as love, her husband saw it as more responsibility and eventually ran into the arms of another woman. At 20, Yvonne was divorced and alone with her child.

By 22 she had remarried. Eric was a good man who seemed to love and care for Yvonne and her son, Scott. They lived in a perfect little house and she was sure life would now be the fairy tale she'd dreamed of. But this story ended not as a dream but as a nightmare when, after two and a half months of marriage, Eric was fatally wounded in an accident. He died after twenty-one days of intensive care.

Everyone told Yvonne she was still young, she'd find another man. She was young, only 22, a mother with two marriages behind her. She did find another man. This man was more like her first husband—he inflicted physical and emotional abuse right from the beginning.

While suffering at home, Yvonne did find comfort in her business. When Eric had died there was enough insurance money for Yvonne to start designing wigs and hairpieces. Her efforts were paying off and she was thinking of opening another shop. But that dream also turned into a nightmare. Just after closing time one evening, Yvonne, waiting for a late customer, was sweeping up the back room when she heard the little bell on the door ring. Thinking it was the customer, she headed to the front, only to find a man with a gun who robbed and then raped her. At first her husband was kind to her because of her ordeal, but then it turned to taunting, and the taunting into threats of what he would do if she ever left him.

Amidst her pain, Yvonne went to the doctor for a physical check-up. Cervical cancer was discovered. At 26, she was told she had five years to live. She had a hysterectomy but it didn't relieve the fear of death and she often thought of suicide. The only comfort she found was in singing a song her grandmother had taught her when she was a child, "Jesus loves me this I know . . . " While the song offered comfort, she didn't really know that Jesus loved her or that He was listening to her cries.

Yvonne didn't die of cancer, and she didn't kill herself, but the abusive marriage ended. She left her little house and started over again. As had become her pattern, Yvonne met a new man. This one was different; this man was a Christian. An eighteen-month courtship developed and Tony led Yvonne to Jesus and eventually to the altar. Yvonne blossomed in the love of God and her new husband.

Yvonne had a new life, but she still had the old hurts, and until the Lord did a healing work in her life, Tony became the focus of her anger.

Your story may not be as long or complex as Yvonne's, or it may have many of the same elements. Perhaps you come from a dysfunctional home or were rejected or abandoned by your parents. You may have been through a difficult or unwanted divorce, or even two or three. You might be the victim of sexual abuse, either as a child or through a violent rape as an adult. In any case, if you have suffered misery in your life, and found like Yvonne that Christ provides healing from your hurts, you also know it doesn't happen overnight.

The process for Yvonne took three years and involved a lot of steps that seemed to go both forward and backward. For Yvonne, the steps the Lord brought her through involved, **first**, learning who Jesus really is and who she is in Him. **Second**, she learned to face the secrets of her past and flush out the repressed feelings. **Third**, Yvonne learned to face her own sin and the way she hurt others because of her pain. **Fourth**, she learned to surrender both her past and her guilt by trusting God. **Fifth**, she learned what forgiveness is and how to forgive herself and others, and receive forgiveness.

Last, Yvonne learned she is in a spiritual battle, and with Jesus she has the tools to fight and win.

After Yvonne had grown both spiritually and emotionally and her marriage was strong, she was asked to share her story. It was for a little church they had been attending. The ladies' group consisted of a handful of saintly looking women, and Yvonne feared that once they knew the truth about her, she would be rejected. God had other plans, and there among these women God turned Yvonne's miseries into a ministry. As she haltingly shared her story, lives were touched and tears were shed, not just for Yvonne but for their own lives as well.

At the conclusion of her presentation, Yvonne asked in prayer for a show of hands of those who could relate to Yvonne's story in any way and each of them raised their hand. When she asked, "Do any of you have unresolved circumstances or feelings from your past that you would like to bring to Jesus for healing?" They again raised their hands.

Here is a likely beginning of a support group, the women's needs had different roots, but they each needed help. Three of the women had been sexually abused, one was a recent widow, one had never dealt with the death of a child and one had never forgiven her husband for leaving her. Every woman in this perfect-looking group had hurts.

This did not become Yvonne's first support group, but it was the start of her personal ministry. She had shared her life and God had used her efforts in the lives of others. God confirmed for Yvonne that she did have something to say and He could use her.

It was at this point in Yvonne's life that I met her. She had been asked to speak to a group of more than a hundred women and she needed some help in putting her story together, so she came to CLASS. She learned about organizing and presenting her story, and she met other women with similar needs. She also received the motivation and direction to continue. She went to that big speaking engagement and again God did a mighty work through her ministry.

At that same time Yvonne's new church was looking to start a ministry to victims. She started attending some of their sessions, and after a few weeks the church leaders came to her and asked her to pray about heading up the ministry and leading a support group. The doors opened and she started with the church ministry. When she set up her first support group, Yvonne really had no models to follow so she used as a guide the steps the Lord had brought her through.

A small group, or support group, ministry is a valuable tool in a person's healing process. The group serves as a support and encourages its members. People who are interested in attending a group are those who don't have the physical, emotional or spiritual resources to move beyond their pain. Some of the things the group's members will learn are: They are not alone in their feelings; they have choices to make about their circumstances; they can move forward beyond their pain; they can have healthy relationships; they can grow in relationship with Jesus.

Through that group, the Lord brought a lot of healing to the women in attendance, even Yvonne. As the women asked questions about their own lives, they revealed issues that were still unsettled in her life. While she was further along in her healing process than the others, she too experienced much growth.

The questions and issues of those in attendance will help you discover what issues are still unresolved for you. The reason to start a support group is for the benefit of those in attendance, but many blessings will come to your own life and personal growth process as a result of your willingness to Give Back.

Looking at your own life and your continued need of a Savior is the best model you can be for those you are helping. Your job isn't to be the healer, but to help others realize their needs and where they have drifted away from God. In being a group facilitator, you aren't saying you are perfect or have resolved all your own issues, but just that you are willing to help others walk through the same ground you have traveled. Yvonne sees this role as being like a windshield wiper: You don't drive the car, you can't stop the rain, but you can help clear the path to avoid future accidents!

Before starting a group type of ministry in your own area, examine your motives to be sure they are pure. Ask God to reveal any secret or impure motive you may harbor for beginning a group like this. If He does reveal some issues in your own life, deal with them first by admitting your own needs. Confess your weaknesses. Risk looking at your own true feelings. Seek your value through Jesus and ask someone, such as your pastor or counselor, to hold you accountable.

Getting Started

Yvonne likens the starting of this type of ministry to the story of the Samaritan woman in the Gospel of John. She was a woman with a past. We know she had five husbands and was living with another man at the time of her encounter with Christ. Her future held no promises and her life was full of disappointments. It was within those disappointments that God could transform her and begin a ministry. So it is with us. Whatever your story, God can use those disappoint-ments in your life to help others.

When she met Jesus, she cried tears of desperation and repentance. We too, cry in desperation and repentance.

When she understood who Jesus was, it changed her forever. He filled her life-long thirst for love and security and He does the same for us.

When she left Jesus to go into the village to tell others about him, she had a ministry. She gave Jesus to others. Her testimony was her credential to minister to others.

If you have a testimony of how Jesus has taken the disappointments of your life, cleansed your tears, healed you with His mighty power, and you now are ready to share with others what Jesus has done for you, you are ready to use your miseries as a ministry.

Pray

As with starting any ministry, Yvonne suggests that you begin a small group ministry with prayer. Specifically, she suggests that you pray that God will you give you direction for your particular group. Ask Him for guidance as to His purpose for the group, who He wants to be reached through it, and what He wants to accomplish in their lives.

Who Will Attend

You may choose to have your group be limited to just those who have been through the same type of experiences you have, such as divorce, sexual abuse or rejection, or you may choose to open the group to all types of victims. Yvonne defines a victim as a person who is stuck in a pattern of thinking, believing they have no choices. While the events that put women into the role of being victims may be very different, they have feelings of rejection, worthlessness and betrayal in common. A support group is especially helpful in dealing with these common feelings.

If you are already involved in counseling or a support group yourself, or if your church has sensed a need for this type of ministry, as Yvonne's church did, you may already have a group of women in need who are just waiting for a leader. In that case the question of who will come and how they will find your group is easy to answer. For those who don't have people begging them to start a group, Yvonne offers these suggestions for creating a group.

Publicly share your story. There are many churches and other women's groups that are in need of programs. Most of them have limited resources from which to pay speakers, but if you have a story of God's victory in your life and you are willing to share it, there will be places for you to go. Some of the established places that always use speakers are Christian Women's Clubs and Women's Aglow. Both of these groups have local meetings in almost every town and they meet once a month. They both have strict guidelines their speakers must follow and the speakers usually have to be approved by the organization. Although they may not be the easiest places to start, both provide a wonderful opportunity for ministry.

Additionally, you can let all your friends and any other churches you have contact with know that you are interested in speaking for their women's group or Bible study groups. When these opportunities do develop for you and you share your testimony, let the audience know of your interest in developing a support group in the upcoming months. *Have a sign-up sheet available* and ask those who would be interested to write down their names, addresses and phone numbers.

A few other ideas for assembling a group are to *create a flyer* announcing the formation of the group, its purpose and location, and who to contact for more information. This flyer can be placed on a display board at church and passed out in the church bulletin. Most Christian bookstores act as clearing houses for information to the local Christian community and are happy to *post announcements* like yours.

Additionally, your flyer could be sent to churches in your local area and individually mailed to anyone you know who might be interested.

Newspapers often have a community news section where they will place notices about activities in the community. Send them a simple *news release* featuring (again) the Who, What, When, Where, Why and How of your group. Don't forget to include the smaller, free community or Christian newspapers your area may offer.

If you try all these approaches at the same time, you may have too many responses for your initial group and you could end up with women who feel hurt or left out, so just try one or two approaches at a time.

Before inviting everyone into the group who wants to attend, Yvonne suggests you establish a screening process and choose for participants those who have similar goals and expectations. She suggests interviewing each potential member and asking yourself the following questions about her:

1. What does she (or he) expect from the group?
2. Is she able to commit to the group and its purpose?
3. Does she seem willing to look at her own issues?
4. What can she contribute to the group as a whole?
5. Is this where God wants her now?

After you talk with each prospective member, pray with her for direction. You will need to sign her up, or place her on a waiting list, or refer her somewhere else.

Yvonne feels that when you have eight to ten women interested in attending, you have enough to start the group. Since not everyone who indicates an interest will actually be available on the selected starting date, you should have a few more names listed than your chosen group's size limit. Yvonne suggests the ideal size for the group be six to eight.

Advisors

Because leading a group can bring up many of your own unresolved issues or become an all-consuming passion for you, Yvonne strongly recommends that you have an advisor before you start your group. This person could be a leader in your church, your counselor or someone who is further along in the recovery process than you are. Choose someone you trust and ask that person to be a mentor or consultant for your group. Meet with this person on a weekly basis to talk about how you are doing and the progress of the group. It is important for us as leaders to have someone to whom we are accountable.

Location

There are many places a group can be held. Of course, within your church is a good place to start. The group could meet in a classroom or an office. Community centers are often open to such groups and libraries or banks also have rooms they open up for community use. To help prevent the group from invading your private life and to limit interruptions, it is best not to have the group meet in your own home.

Whatever site you choose, you should meet in the same place every week so no one gets lost in the moving. The location should comfortably seat the number of people expected and be private enough to foster intimate discussions.

Content

Now you are ready to actually get started with your group, so you'll need to plan what you are going to do during the sessions. Yvonne has spent five years leading support groups through her church and the last three years teaching others how to lead groups themselves. She has developed an entire guide book for leading support groups and, while it is not published at the time of this writing, it is available directly through Yvonne. I would encourage you to contact her and get a copy of her guide before starting your own group.

Whether you choose to create your own format, follow an existing workbook or use Yvonne's guide book, I believe you will find the following framework from Yvonne's experience to be helpful.

Each session should have a balance of teaching, discussion and prayer. In John 8:12 Jesus says, "I am the light of the world; he who follows me will not walk in darkness." Teaching the truths in God's word helps correct inaccurate beliefs about God and how He feels about us. The teaching must reinforce that truth about who Jesus is and who we are in Him.

Discussion allows the group to understand how the members feel about themselves and God. As a part of the discussion time, Yvonne suggests allowing "cross-talk." This means that when someone else is talking, other members are allowed to make comments. While some well known groups do not allow this type of interaction because of fear of criticism and advice-giving, Yvonne has found that with some basic guidelines, cross-talk allows the support and interaction that makes a group work.

The guidelines she suggests are:

1. No gossip; each person is there to work on his (or her) own problems, not someone else's.

2. No judging; avoiding comments that condemn or criticize.

3. No interruptions; allow each person to completely express his feelings, whether it be through talking, crying, expressing anger, or whatever.

It is the facilitator's job to stop inappropriate conversations and bring them to the group's attention.

Prayer is important because it allows the members not only to receive, but also to give. Prayer invites every member to become an ambassador of Jesus Christ by ministering His grace and love. Every question, conflict or problem should be taken to the feet of Jesus. This invites hearts to be open and to receive healing, and it takes the focus off us and puts it directly on the Healer, Jesus.

Week by Week

This week-by-week section is Yvonne's suggested format for a typical eight-week program.

Week #1—Welcome

This is the time for welcomes and getting acquainted. Each member should fill out an intake form (see sample on next page), and exchange names and phone numbers for follow-up. The leader shares her goals and objectives and what is expected from each participant. This enables the group members to know what they can expect from the group experience.

Week #2—Know God

Most hurting people struggle with low self-esteem and rejection, and with those damaged personal reflections our image of God is usually distorted as well. Week two begins

---

INTAKE CARD

DATE _

NAME _

ADDRESS _

           CITY _ _ _ _ _ _ _ _ _ _ _ ZIP _ _ _ _ _ _ _ _ _

TELEPHONE NUMBER DAYS _ _ _ _ _ _ EVENINGS _ _ _ _ _ _

         BEST TIME TO CALL YOU _ _ _ _ _ _ _ _ _ _ _ _

EMPLOYER _

ADDRESS _

SINGLE _ MARRIED _ DIVORCED _ WIDOWED _ OTHER _ _

PERSON TO CALL IN CASE OF EMERGENCY _ _ _ _ _ _ _ _ _

ADDRESS _

CITY _ _ _ _ _ _ _ _ _ _ _ _ _ _ ZIP _ _ _ _ _ TELEPHONE _ _ _ _ _

Concerning Confidentiality:

The undersigned understands that his/her case may be shared with (your church, pastor, or counseling staff) strictly on a confidential basis, unless specific refusal by you is voiced. The purpose of any discussion is to allow us to pray about your concerns and help one another deal with problems such as yours.

In cases concerning the abuse of children, the elderly, corporal harm to another or yourself, we are legally bound (by your state or other officials) to notify the proper authorities.

      Client Signature _

                 Date _ _ _ _ _ _ _ _ _ _ _ _ _ _ _

Group Name _

Group Leader _

---

with knowing Christ as our source for healing. Clearing up wrong thinking about God is essential to recovery.

Week #3—Self-Examination . . . Repressed Secrets

In this safe environment, the group's members look at the emotions they have never had an opportunity to feel. Since the initial events and attached feelings have become unspoken secrets, sharing feels risky and painful. This may be a time of tears, anger and denial but openness is essential to wholeness.

Week #4—Self-Examination . . . Revealed Sins

While victims are not responsible for what was done to them, they are responsible for their reaction to the victimization. Week four gives the members an opportunity to take responsibility for the sins that they have justified because of the pain they feel. Some of the sins that may need to be dealt with are anger, unforgiveness, hatred and abuse.

Week #5—Surrender

The previous weeks have made the members aware of the sins that have been done to them and their sins as a result of those actions. In week five the group members surrender the combined sins to God. At this time Yvonne asks the group members to trust God with their past and give up their need to further punish themselves and others. This is done through prayer—but only when a person is ready . . . when that person is really sick and tired of being sick and tired. This process requires an emptying of the inner man. Not everyone may be ready for this step at this time.

Week #6—Forgiveness

When we have surrendered our sins to Jesus, it opens the pathway for real forgiveness. Four parts of forgiveness should be addressed: (1) forgiving our perpetrator; (2) forgiving ourselves; (3) asking forgiveness of those we have hurt; and (4) reconciling our anger with God. This is done through prayer, and group members pray as they are ready.

Week #7—Recognize the Enemy

With all of the hurt that is evident within a group, the warfare raging around us cannot be ignored. The members have an opportunity to share their fears, nightmares and phobias. Week seven demonstrates God's power to defeat the enemy by looking at what Satan does to hold us captive and at his part in our decision to stay a victim or become a soldier.

Week #8—Conclusion

Group members examine the growth that has taken place in their own lives during the past weeks and offer prayers of praise to God for His faithfulness and healing. They fill out an evaluation of the group, and this is when you determine which ones may wish to repeat the group.

Yvonne has available a suggested format of what each week's activities might cover.

Additional Concerns

Some of the additional concerns that you as a leader need to know about are *your legal responsibility, confidentiality* and the *group's composition.*

It is your duty to keep the details of the member's personal lives in strict confidence, but there are some legal obligations you may face. Your church or state may require you to report instances such as any abuse of a minor, or of elderly or dependent adults, and any threat of suicide or corporal harm. Check with the officials at your church and the state's child protective agencies to see if you are mandated to report any suspicion or knowledge of abuse. The intake form clearly notifies the participants that this may happen. If someone refuses to sign that portion of the form, Yvonne suggests that, for your own protection, they not be permitted to attend the group.

Regarding the group's composition, you may choose to allow both men and women to attend, or you may limit it to just men or just women. While both sexes will have many of the same issues to face, Yvonne has found that a mixed group hinders the level of intimacy and emotional freedom desired. Additionally, the open sexual discussions may tempt the members into sexual sins.

The group may be held in an open or closed format. The open format means that members can come and go without a continued commitment to the group or its facilitator. This type of group is usually designed to be an outreach and does not attain the level of intimacy and trust typical of a closed group. A closed group usually meets for a predesignated length of time, four to twelve weeks, and opens between terms to allow new members to join and existing members to discontinue. For real healing to take place, a closed group is generally more effective.

The information presented here is a condensation and adaptation of Yvonne's book, *Making Ministries From Miseries.* I hope it has given you a good understanding of the basics involved in starting your own small group ministry. Your story may be different, like the woman from Samaria, but if Jesus has changed your life, whether you are fully healed or still in process, you can have a ministry.

To contact Yvonne directly and request further information regarding her workshops on leading support groups, or other speaking, or regarding her book, please send a self-addressed, stamped envelope to:

> Yvonne Martinez
> c/o CLASS
> 1645 S. Rancho Santa Fe, #102
> San Marcos, CA 92069

11

Happiness on a Shoestring

*If any one has the world's goods
and sees his brother in need,
yet closes his heart against him,
how does God's love abide in him?
(1 John 3:17)*

As a young girl in a poor farming community in rural Alabama, Bonnie had a happy home but very few of the things we think of as necessities today. When her shoes wore out, she had to make them last longer. If the soles came unstitched and flapped as she walked, rubber bands were placed around the toe section to hold the bottom on. When her shoestrings broke, she tied them together and kept using them until they finally broke so many times there wasn't enough left to tie. It was there Bonnie first learned to be happy "on a shoestring."

Bonnie had a goal: to get out of that country community and make it in the big city. She worked her way through college with a variety of jobs including part-time secretary to the college registrar, selling class rings for which she got $1.00 per sale, and doing bulletins each Saturday for two churches. Within three years Bonnie got a degree in business and went to work for a senator in Washington, D.C. She was out of Alabama and into the big city!

There Bonnie met and married her husband and she started a long journey of military living. They had three children and moved twenty-two times before her husband retired as a colonel and settled down in San Antonio. By then the children were grown and out of college and Bonnie had some time for herself. Many women in her position would have chosen to relax by playing golf and attending teas, but Bonnie was tired of that and decided to go back to work. First she went to school to brush up on her skills, and then she got a job on one of the military bases in San Antonio, Texas.

Bonnie eventually became the secretary to the Command Surgeon of an air force base in San Antonio. Her boss is responsible for the health and welfare of the entire command and Bonnie believes God put her there for a special purpose.

All day long people come by the office. Many of these people are dealing with difficulties in their personal lives but they do not want their problems to become part of their medical records. However, they freely confide their concerns and frustrations to Bonnie. She is a good listener and she offers advice where she can. In any given day she may listen to five to ten different stories about people's lives.

Most of the women co-workers Bonnie came into contact with were single parents. When they walked through the halls they kept their heads down and the general office morale was low. One day the load seemed particularly heavy and when she returned to her desk from a break, she rested her head on her hands and said, "Dear God, what can I do to help these people realize there is more to life than looking forward to Fridays?" Her prayer was actually more of a question than a prayer, and she didn't really expect an answer.

Three hours later when the Lord answered Bonnie's plea, she had nearly forgotten about asking. Suddenly she knew what she could do to help these people with whom she came in daily contact. The Lord planted an entire concept in her mind and she began to write down the ideas as fast as she could. Within just a few minutes she had several sheets of paper filled and her ideas clearly outlined.

She would start a retreat. Not a big retreat like the Southern California Women's Retreat; in fact, it would be something totally different. These retreats would be called "Happiness on a Shoestring," and they would be in her own home. They would be offered in a series of three weekends, not three weekends in a row, but the first weekend in the month for three months. In the first one she would teach on "the mind" and encourage the women in attendance to use their minds more. The second weekend retreat would be on "the soul" and would involve spiritual reflections. The third would be "the body" and include discussions on color, wardrobe and make-up and a special individual consulting session with a hairdresser.

Bonnie talked to her husband about her idea and he was supportive. Then she presented her plan to some of the women and they were excited.

Her husband agreed to help Bonnie prepare the house and create enough beds so everyone would have a place to sleep. When the day came for the first retreat, Bonnie's husband moved to the Visiting Officers Quarters on base for the night and left the house to the women.

The first retreat was in July of 1988. Since that time Bonnie has offered her retreat three or four times a year. She has seen the entire attitude of her office building change and even the women's appearance has improved and been updated since the retreats. Bonnie has even been honored by the air force base as "Civilian of the Year" for her work.

Evangelism is one of the retreat's subtle goals and while not everything that is covered in the retreats is overtly Christian, Bonnie has seen many women come to the Lord and return to church attendance.

Through the Happiness on a Shoestring Retreats Bonnie has started a "Secret Pal Club" for the women who have attended. There are more than seventy members in the Secret Pal Club and they get together once a year for a special party to reveal whose pal they were and to pick new ones.

Bonnie's home is big enough to have twenty women spend the night. Some sleep on sofas and others on cots but they all have a place. She invites the women from her office building, and their friends, to attend. She is making a difference in her little corner of San Antonio, Texas.

You could take advantage of all the planning and trial and error that Bonnie has gone through. Even if you don't have a house big enough or a husband who is willing to be kicked out once in a while, you could put on a Happiness on a Shoestring Retreat for the women of your community in your church. Your retreat might have a few different features depending on your areas of interest and the experts you have available to help with the teaching. It could be like a big slumber party and would be an excellent way for a smaller church to reach the women in the surrounding area.

Getting Started

If you would like to offer Happiness on a Shoestring Retreats to the women in your church or community, the two things you need to determine first are who will come and where it will be held. You could have the retreats in your home as Bonnie does, or if your home is not large enough, you can have it at your church. If the church has a sanctuary with removable chairs or a multi-use room, that could be a perfect location for a Happiness on a Shoestring Slumber Party. Each woman in attendance could bring a sleeping bag and her own pillow and everyone could sleep in the one big room. That would take care of your location.

Next you need to think about who will attend. Since this style of ministry is limited to about fifteen to twenty women, it is an excellent way for a smaller church to get started in a women's ministry. If there are fifty to sixty women in regular attendance at the church, there are enough to have a Happiness on a Shoestring Retreat or Slumber Party. If you are going to put the retreats on without the support or cooperation of a church, the women might be the mothers of the children in a local school or from your place of employment as in Bonnie's case. You might even mail flyers announcing the event to all the homes in a neighborhood where there are apt to be women in need of such an opportunity. Referrals from friends are a great source of attenders.

Promotion

If you are offering the retreats through a church, the promotion will be easy. It should be announced in the bulletin and promoted from the pulpit. When you present the retreats on your own, you will want to create an invitation to pass out to your targeted audience. The announcement or invitation will need to list the pertinent information that prospects will need to make a decision to come: the dates of all three weekends, times, location and cost, with an outline of the types of materials that will be covered each weekend. Bonnie says the ladies do not need to make a commitment to attend all three weekends, although it would be good for the weekends to build upon each other and have the same group at each one. The invitation should have a registration form, or you could ask the women to call to reserve their space so you know how many to prepare for. Be sure to include either the address for mailing in a reservation or the phone number to call.

Costs

If you are financially able, you may want to cover the costs yourself but Bonnie suggests having a minimal fee of ten or fifteen dollars. She says the weekend will have more value to the women if there is a charge, and I have found this to be true in my years of working with women. The small charge is used to cover the obvious costs of food and printing. Bonnie absorbs the lesser costs of phone calls and postage herself. You could do that or you could increase the fee a couple of additional dollars to cover all the costs.

Meals

Since the retreats don't start until 8 on Friday evening Bonnie doesn't have to provide an evening meal. When the women arrive she has snacks and beverages available. On Saturday morning she serves a breakfast casserole which she has made the day before, frozen bagels which she offers toasted, fresh fruit and orange juice. For the lunches she serves a chicken salad, pizza, or some other food which she can prepare ahead of time, with canned soft drinks or iced tea. She sets up her meals like a buffet by placing a cloth over her washer and dryer, spreading the food out and allowing each lady to serve herself. They eat outside in the back yard. The retreats are scheduled to be over by 4 on Saturday afternoon so breakfast and lunch are the only meals she needs to consider. The whole thing is simple and casual, but that is part of what creates a bond among the women who attend.

Schedule

All three weekends starting at 8 Friday evening and ending at 4 Saturday afternoon allows single moms the best opportunity to get away since they will need to find overnight child care for only one evening.

I am including here the basic schedule Bonnie uses for her three retreats.

Week #1— The Mind

Goal—to help each woman who attends to realize and feel she is special and to challenge her to use her mind to broaden her horizons.

FRIDAY EVENING

8:00-9:00 Welcoming participants and encouraging them to get acquainted.

Bonnie gives each women a name tag that has only her first name listed. She wants the focus of the weekend to be on the women rather than on their families. Bonnie tells a little of her life story, especially how she learned to use her mind and her desire for education as a way of letting the women know where she is coming from and to get them thinking about their lives.

Then she has each person introduce herself but tells them not to talk about their families, only themselves. After the introductions everyone gets into their bedclothes for the rest of the evening's activities.

9:00-10:00 Games and other fun activities that will begin to stimulate the mind.

Bonnie likes to use the Un-Game. Although she doesn't use the board because the group is too big, she does use the question cards and it provides an excellent way for the women to begin sharing.

10:00-11:00 A time of encouragement before bed.

As one example, Bonnie facilitates this by giving each women an empty box, some silver wrapping paper and a bow. After they have wrapped their boxes, she asks them to lean back and listen to a tape, "Silver Boxes, The Gift of Encouragement," by my mother, Florence Littauer, Bonnie says that each woman usually gives her box to one of the other ladies with a word of encouragement for that person before going to bed. If you are concerned that the women who attend your group might not want to do that, you could structure the giving of encouragement by having each person draw the name of one of the women and have her give that woman her box with the word of encouragement or a compliment. Even if the ladies don't all know each other, they can still offer an encouraging word such as, "I love your night gown," or "You have a wonderful smile." This assures that each person ends up with a box other than her own and goes to bed with an encouraging word. Since many people never hear any encouragement in their lives, this is an excellent way to end the evening.

SATURDAY

7:45-9:00 A.M. Breakfast.

While this meal is being eaten Bonnie has some classical or inspiring music playing to set a relaxing tone.

9:00-10:00 Teaching hour.

Bonnie shares the concepts of the birth orders from *The Birth Order Book* by Kevin Leman. She tells about her birth order and how it has affected her life. With the remaining time she asks the women to share anything that has come to their minds about their birth order and its effects on their lives. Bonnie says they can get so excited about this subject that it could take up the rest of the day, so be careful to stay close to the schedule. The first time she did this retreat, they had such fun talking about the birth order concepts, they got totally off schedule and almost missed lunch.

10:00-12:00 Personality study.

Next Bonnie moves into a study of the personalities to continue giving the women an increased understanding of who they are. She gives an overview of the subject from the books *Personality Plus* and *Your Personality Tree* by Florence Littauer. She has each woman take the personality profile while she reads them the word definitions from the back of "Your Personality Tree" in one of the books.

12:00-1:00 Lunch.

The women are encouraged to discuss their personalities with each other.

1:00-2:00 Sharing and discussion.

Everyone shares the results of their personality profiles and they discuss how their personalities have affected their lives.

2:00-3:00 Suggestions for follow-up activities.

Books supporting the topics presented during the retreat are reviewed and places the women can go to and things they can do within the local area that are free and educational are presented. Bonnie encourages the women to continue to read and put good things into their mind. Some of the books she suggests within the structure of the first week are:

Florence Littauer	*Make the Tough Times Count*
	Silver Boxes
	How to get Along With Difficult People
	After Every Wedding Comes a Marriage
	Personality Plus
	Your Personality Tree
	Blow Away the Black Clouds
	Hope for Hurting Women
	It Takes So Little to Be Above Average
	Raising Christians—Not Just Children
Fred and Florence Littauer	*Freeing Your Mind*
	From Memories That Bind
Fred Littauer	*The Promise of Restoration*
Dr. Kevin Leman	*The Birth Order Book*
	Unlocking the Secrets of Childhood Memories
Dr. Norman Vincent Peale	*The Power of Joy*
	and Enthusiasm
Dale Carnegie	*How to Win Friends*
	and Influence People
Jan Frank	*Door of Hope*
Derek Prince	*Blessing or Curse*
Dr. Robert Schuller	*Tough Times Never Last;*
	Tough People Do

3:00-4:00 Victory Logs.

Each woman creates a "Victory Log" for herself. This is a notebook that she begins there at the retreat and is encouraged to continue to keep up in the following months. In her Victory Log each woman starts by writing all the good things in her life and adds to it every day by entering the good things that happen that day. This motivates each person to focus on the positive things in her life and offers her a resource for encouragement when she's feeling down.

4:00 Closing time.

All the attenders sit in a circle holding hands. Bonnie tells them all that they are special and then each person takes turns sharing why she is special. At the close Bonnie plays a tape of Whitney Houston's song, "The Greatest Love of All," and they all sing along with it. Bonnie ends the weekend with a prayer of thanks to which everyone is invited to contribute.

Week #2—The Soul

Goal—To show the attenders that while it is important to love themselves and feel special, they also need the love of God.

FRIDAY EVENING

8:00-9:00 Welcome and refreshments.

Following the same format as the first session, Bonnie tells some of her story focusing on her spiritual journey and asks each person to introduce herself since some of the women in attendance may be different from the previous session.

9:00-10:30 Games and fellowship.

Like the first weekend, Friday evening is spent in a time of fun and fellowship. They usually play some games and frequently use the Un-Game again.

10:30-11:00 Devotions.

Bonnie shares a devotional and closes the evening with a time of prayer.

SATURDAY

7:45-9:00 Breakfast.

9:00-10:00 Teaching hour.

Using large charts, Bonnie presents a discussion of the world's great religions with a special emphasis on Christianity to give the women an overview of what is out there.

10:00-11:00 Sharing time.

Following the discussion on religion, Bonnie presents a review of the Christian denominations and provides an opportunity for each person to share about her childhood religion or denomination and about her current church. Bonnie asks them to share what their church is doing to help hurting women. She finds many of them don't know there are churches that offer things like support groups and counseling.

11:00-12:00 Quiet hour.

In this hour Bonnie asks each person to spend some time alone. They spread out through the house and yard for an hour of meditation and reflection. She gives each person a collection of materials to reflect upon, which might include poems and Scriptures to help them focus. She also provides each person with a list of the names and addresses of Christian bookstores in the area and a list of additional suggested readings. At the end of the hour, after they have read over the provided literature, they are requested to write down their individual philosophy of life. Many of the women have never thought of such a thing before, and this time always proves to be a highlight of the retreat. Bonnie plays classical music to help set the mood during this time.

12:00-1:00 Lunch.

This offers the women a chance to discuss their ideas.

1:00-2:00 Sharing.

Each woman shares her newly written philosophy with the group and they all discuss them.

2:00-4:00 Suggestions for follow-up activities.
            Secret Pal Club.

The group has a discussion of ways they can reach out to others and be better witnesses. Then Bonnie introduces the Secret Pal Club and each woman draws from a basket the name of a woman who will be her secret pal for the next year. Women leave packages and cards on Bonnie's desk for their secret pals and Bonnie calls the pal to let her know she has something to pick up. In closing, the women all join hands in a circle and pray for their secret pal and any additional needs or concerns that have come up during their time together.

Week #3—The Body

Goal—To encourage the women to take better care of themselves through proper diet, exercise, dress and attitude.

FRIDAY EVENING

8:00-9:00 Welcome.

Following the format of the previous weekends, the women are welcomed and introduced.

9:00-10:00 Exercise.

Depending on the location and the weather, everyone goes for a walk or a swim or does some light aerobics or stretching exercises to get them into the mind-set of taking care of themselves and improving their appearance.

10:00-11:00 Fellowship and devotions.

The group plays games and sings songs that involve physical activity. Bonnie closes the session with a short devotional and prayer asking God to help them all realize the importance of taking care of their bodies.

SATURDAY

7:45-9:00 Breakfast.

9:00-10:00 Teaching hour.

Bonnie introduces them to concepts of looking good and feeling better, reminding each person that her body is a temple of God.

10:00-12:00 Demonstration.

Demonstration on color and wardrobe is done either by a specialist in that field or through the use of teaching videos.

12:00-1:00 Lunch.

1:00-2:30 Discussion.

Make-up and style are discussed, again either through the use of a local expert in the field or teaching videos.

2:30-4:00 Beauty analyses.

Bonnie invites her hairdresser to come, and each woman gets a turn having her face shape and hair texture analyzed. The hairdresser makes suggestions for each person as to what type of style would be right for her based on her individual features and needs.

4:00 Closing.

The time is closed with all the women joined together in a circle for prayer.

This schedule is flexible and serves as a framework for the weekends' activities.

The Happiness on a Shoestring Retreats end on Saturday afternoon, but their effect goes on. After her first one, Bonnie could see a difference in the lives of the women who had attended. They had learned about themselves, made some new friends, and had an opportunity to get away to a new environment and concentrate solely on their own needs. Soon others were asking when Bonnie was going to offer another retreat so they could come, too.

Additional Suggestions

Don't feel you need to be an expert in all the areas you want to have covered in the retreat sessions. You can alter some of the topics from the exact format Bonnie uses if you have expertise in other areas. If you are not familiar with the material on birth order or personalities but you have other information you are excited about that has really helped you understand yourself better, present that instead. Just make whatever adjustments needed to make it work for you.

You can bring in experts from your community to help with the sessions where you may be weaker. For example if there is a chiropractor within your church or your circle of friends, you might want to have her come in during the sessions on the body and have her teach the basics of good posture.

If you have someone who sells make-up, she may be willing to come in and present the session on make-up. If you do use some of these outside experts, you'll want to be sure they understand this is not a time for open selling.

Bonnie keeps a wide selection of support materials in stock that includes the books and tapes she uses and those she recommends, and she has them available for the women to purchase during the weekend so they can continue their learning. Most of the books are Christian books and they continue to witness to the women after the women have gone home.

There are breaks interspersed throughout the weekend's schedule and Bonnie uses sing-a-longs to help create a spirit of unity and to give the women a sense of roots and of history through traditional folk songs.

Take lots of polaroid pictures of the women during the weekends and give them some of the pictures of themselves to take home as reminders of the time and of the commitments they have made.

Bonnie also uses a video camera to tape the women, especially during the sessions on the body, so they can see how they come across to others. She shows them the tapes while they are there. At each retreat a photo album is displayed full of pictures of past events.

And a newsletter helps keep the ladies in touch.

Further Ministry

Bonnie held her first Happiness on a Shoestring Retreat in 1988. She didn't know where it might go or what God would choose to do with it, but she followed His directions for her at the time. It was such a success and the lives of the women were touched in such a way that others were soon asking if they could come too. Since that time, Bonnie has offered the retreats two or three times a year and added some special one-day seminars on subjects she found to be of special interest to the women in attendance. These have been on subjects such as: "Hospitality on a Shoestring," "Decorating on a Shoestring," and "Raising Happy Children on a Shoestring."

One memorable project for Bonnie's group in San Antonio was an all-day backyard bazaar where the ladies sold their own creations from booths. In addition, parties and showers are held to honor individuals throughout the year. The ladies affectionately refer to themselves as the "Shoestring Girls."

Bonnie plans to continue offering the retreats and seminars to the women of her community as long as there is an interest. The retreats have a powerful impact on the lives of women who are not getting help, motivation or training from traditional sources and Bonnie hopes other women throughout the country will be challenged to this type of ministry opportunity as well.

Does this sound like a way for you to Give Back? Is this a ministry opportunity you would like to start through your church or in your own home? Bonnie's story may help you capture the vision for this project. You can take her ideas and use them as a springboard for creating your own Happiness on a Shoestring Retreat, or you can get more help from Bonnie. She has a complete notebook available with all the information on putting on the retreats with copies of all the handouts. If you would like information regarding these materials, contact Bonnie at the address below. Please enclose a self-addressed, stamped envelope for your reply.

Bonnie Skinner
Happiness on a Shoestring Retreats
7111 Stirrup Circle
San Antonio, TX 78240

Section I I I
Obligation

*I can do all things
in Him
who strengthens me
(Philippians 4:13).*

12

Listening

I will instruct you and guide you
(says the Lord)
along the best pathway for your life;
I will advise you and watch your progress
(Psalm 32:8).

"I would like to know how you trained your ear to hear God's voice." Those words played themselves in my mind over and over again. I don't know who said them—they were written anonymously on a seminar evaluation form. But for me, I knew they were from God. They were His voice speaking to me through another person's writing.

A friend and I had been teaching a seminar. As we always did, we had asked for those in attendance to fill out an evaluation form at the end so that we could continue to grow and could improve our material. People commented on the parts of our program that were the most helpful to them and what parts they would have liked more of. In general they said kind, flattering things that made us think

we were on the right track and that this seminar was where
God wanted us to be. We were still in the stage of throwing
the seeds on the ground and asking God to provide the
increase. This particular seminar, our fifth one, was the first
we had been invited to and were paid for. The previous four
had been for practice, presented free to audiences I had
called. We were excited to have this paying engagement.
The evaluations were positive and we began thinking of
putting the material into a book.

Those were our plans, but we learned they were not
God's plans. We had presented the program to more than
five hundred women. Each had gone home with several
handouts from the session. On all the handouts were our
names, addresses and phone numbers so they could reach
us if they wanted us to come to another group with the same
seminar. We were on Southern California's largest Christian
radio station talking about this seminar, letting people know
we were available to come to their church. We went on
nationwide Christian television and presented the concepts
of the seminar, again to encourage people to invite us to
their churches with it.

We did everything we could to promote the program.
We tossed the seeds out—but they never grew. That fifth
seminar we did was our last.

We had believed the concepts for that seminar came
to us from God. But I have learned that many people get
ideas they believe are from God. Sometimes they are. Sometimes they are not. How can you tell? How can you learn to
hear God's voice?

I wondered myself, and after that last seminar, that one
comment from the evaluations kept coming back to me: "I
would like to know how you trained your ear to hear God's
voice." I doubt my friend even remembers the comment,
but I recognized God's voice.

I have always felt God's direction in my life. It isn't that I am so highly spiritual I hear voices all the time, but as I look back over where I have been and what I have done, I see God's plan. Sometimes He directed by events like opening and closing doors. Sometimes it was through other people who wrote or said things I just knew were sent from God to me. Other times it was directly through Scripture and the words nearly jumped off the pages and hit me in the face so I couldn't ignore them. At times it was even a voice so loud and clear in my head that I had to look around the room to see if others were hearing it too. Yes, I knew I heard God's voice, but for me it was nothing I'd learned; it was something that just happened.

But still those words replayed: "I'd like to know how you trained your ear to hear God's voice."

"How did I?"

I asked Him.

And I kept asking, "How did I learn?" For me it wasn't a loud or verbal plea. It wasn't through written prayer, although I surely believe in that. It was a constant thought that I was aware of. I just quietly replayed in my mind, "How did I learn?" God wouldn't let the thought die.

He answered in the same ways I had learned before to expect His direction in my life: through the words of someone else, events that happened, Scripture I just knew was there that day for me, a voice so loud and clear I couldn't ignore it.

Our last seminar had been in June. In July I went to the Christian Booksellers' Convention as I usually do. Since a new book of my mother's was being released by Word Publishing, we spent quite a bit of time at the Word booth. They had on display another new book, by Bob Benson. It was called *He Speaks Softly,* subtitled *Learning to Hear*

God's Voice. When I saw that book I thought, *Ah! There's my answer. I'll get this book and find out how I learned to hear God's voice, and then I'll give a seminar on it.* The gentlemen at the Word booth gave me a copy.

From the Christian Bookseller's Convention my mother and I were to go directly to the National Speakers Association Convention in Washington, D.C. At the end of the Booksellers' Convention someone offered us a free ride to the airport. They had rented a limousine and there was room for us—the only snag was, we had to leave four hours early. Being the types who love both bargains and luxury, we accepted the offer, packed quickly and took the free limo ride to the airport.

Since my mother nearly lives in airports, she is a life member in American Airlines Admirals Club. We arrived at National Airport four hours before our flight. The airport was dirty, congested and noisy, but as we stepped through the doors of the Admirals Club it was like a different world. The ceilings were low and the room was dark. Low leather chairs sat invitingly around in the room and each one had a reading light over it. The hush throughout reminded me of a library. My mother chose one of the empty desks along the wall and sat down to write thank you notes; I chose a chair for reading. I settled in, reached for my new book and started.

There I was, removed from the hustle and bustle of the world, focused on "Learning to hear God's voice." I wasn't actually praying, but I was focused and searching. After I had read about six pages, God spoke to me. It was in one of those clear, loud voices, and I did look around the room. No one else seemed to have heard anything. I listened.

God gave me four distinct points regarding how I had learned to hear His voice. I got my organizer out of my purse and wrote down those four steps. Then I began reading again. When I had read about a third of the book, I realized it was Bob Benson's story and not really a "how-to" book. Realizing it was going a different direction from what I wanted at the moment, I quit reading and put it away for a while.

Months later a church called and invited me to speak. They asked what topic I would like to speak on, so I suggested "Learning to Hear God's Voice." They liked the idea and we set a date, some months away.

In true Sanguine fashion, I had never written this new speech—but I had those four points God had given me back in Washington safely nestled in my organizer, right where I had put them. The Thursday evening before I was to speak to that group on Saturday it dawned on me: "If I am going to write this new speech, this is the time to do it." I was working all day Friday and having company for dinner Friday evening. Thursday night had to be it.

I got out my organizer, my Bible with a concordance, and a note pad. I looked in the concordance for verses to back up the points God had given me. There were so many it was hard to narrow them down to just a few. Those four points were definitely of God. They were everywhere in Scripture. As I read my Bible that evening, God spoke to me again—this time through His Word. So many verses that all seemed to say the same thing kept leaping off the pages and grabbing my attention. Through those verses, God increased my understanding of how I had learned to hear His voice. The four points God showed me are discussed in the next chapter of this book.

While I can't guarantee they will work for you, I can promise they are God's plan for hearing His voice. They are repeated in His Word over and over again. His Word is there to speak to me and to you.

Lord teach me to listen. The times are noisy
and my ears are weary with the thousand

raucous sounds which continuously assault them. Give me the spirit of the boy Samuel when he said, "Speak for thy servant heareth." Let me hear Thee speaking in my heart. Let me get used to the sound of Thy voice, that its tones may be familiar when the sounds of the earth die away and the only sound will be the music of Thy speaking. Amen.

A. W. Tozer[1]

13

Complete Confidence Through the Vital Union

I will put my confidence in you.
Yes, I will trust the promises of God
(Psalm 56:3, TLB).

I had thought the seminar my friend and I taught was from God. I had gotten the idea for it like a brainstorm. I told my friend about it and she too thought it was a great idea so we proceeded in putting together materials and giving practice seminars. God closed the door. I have never given that seminar again.

Learning to Hear God's Voice

Those points God gave me about learning to hear His voice have become my favorite presentation and it is the one people invite me to give most often. God opened that door.

As you have read the ideas presented in this book, you may have felt God speaking to you about a ministry that is right for you. You are ready to Give Back. God may have spoken to you about one of the exact ministries presented here, or maybe He has given you an entirely new idea as to what you can do to make a difference in your community. Before you embark on this new opportunity, you'll want to check to see if, indeed, your ideas are God's ideas.

This is what I learned.

1. Know God

First we have to **know God.** Rather than just knowing He is up there somewhere, we also must have a close, personal, daily communion with Him. We must have made a commitment to Him and invited Him into our lives at some point. I have learned God doesn't talk to strangers. John 10:14-16 says:

> I am the Good Shepherd and know my own sheep
> and they know me . . . and they will heed my voice
> and there will be one flock with one Shepherd (TLB).

I knew God; I was a part of His flock. I had given my life to Him when I was 9 years old. I was in the hospital about to have my tonsils out when my father shared the Four Spiritual Laws booklet with me. At the end it asked, "Is there any reason why you wouldn't want to invite Christ into your life right now?"

I couldn't see any.

I had seen my parents change through going to a new church and becoming Christians. My sister had become a Christian. Now it was my turn. I invited Christ into my life.

When I was 19, I prayed for direction in my life. I heard God's voice through a series of events that gave me that desired direction. In college I majored in interior design. As I got into the advanced classes I discovered I didn't have the patience it took to do a complete custom project. The furniture might be late because the dock workers went on strike; the drapes could come and be too short, or the custom fabrics made from different dye lots and would have to be sent back; I would be sick of the people and the entire project. I'd want to redecorate before I ever finished.

So I prayed, "God, what do you want me to do with the natural talent and the education I have?" My search coincided with my mother and Emilie Barnes' search. At that time they were teaching classes together. They were sort of all-purpose, get-your-act-together classes. In those classes they presented the idea of "having your colors done" as a means of "organizing your wardrobe."

The women who attended their seminars could see the value in this concept and wanted to have their colors done. After a while the woman my mother and Emilie were sending people to became so busy in that activity that she didn't have the time to work with the ladies, so they began searching for someone to replace her.

One day my mother said to me, "Marita, you have a good eye for color and you love working with women. Why don't you learn to do this color analysis? Then you can travel and speak with us."

She was right. I did love to go with them, and I had frequently joined them anyway just to help pass out papers— so I set out to learn color analysis.

This was many years ago now, before anyone had really ever heard of having their colors done. God opened doors and answered my prayers for direction in my life. I got some training and developed my own program. The area of color analysis proved successful for me. I worked with clients seven days a week. When I was 23, Harvest House publishers asked me to write a book on the subject and *Shades of Beauty* became the first book in Christian publishing on color analysis. I spoke to women's groups across the country; I drove a nice car and had several pieces of real estate.

Yes, God opened many doors for me and I knew I was where He wanted me. But after a while I became too busy doing what I knew God wanted me to do to spend any time with Him. I didn't spend much time in prayer and while I meant to spend time reading my Bible, it never quite happened. I still knew Him, I was still a Christian, but I didn't really *know* Him.

One day my business collapsed. It was as if my phone had been disconnected. No one called to make appointments to have their colors done anymore. I didn't know how to do anything else, and I cried out to God to save my business. I thought, *God, this is where You put me. What has happened? I thought You wanted me here.*

He didn't answer.

I had become like the Israelites in Deuteronomy. They were doing well; life was good; they didn't need God. Deuteronomy 8:11 says: "Beware that in your plenty you don't forget the Lord your God" (TLB). I was in my plenty and I had forgotten my Lord, my God.

If you are looking for God's direction in your life, you have got to know Him more than just knowing He is around and more than just having invited Him into your life. You must know Him like a best friend, someone with whom you are in constant contact.

If you have never invited Christ into your life, go through the section entitled "Would You Like to Know God Personally?" at the end of this book. When you get to the end, pray the prayer that is suggested there like I did when I was 9. Christ will come into your life as He promised, and you will become a Christian. Then you can set out to get to know God and prepare for Him to offer you deep insights and direction for your life.

If you are a new Christian, or are an old one who, like me, lost touch with God in your time of plenty, you need to get started in really knowing Him.

If you already have that close intimate relationship with God, that is wonderful! You already may have found close communion with Him and you may know that where you now are is where He wants you.

That close communion comes from spending time with Him daily. In his book, *You Gotta Keep Dancin'*, Tim Hansel says,

> I was asked not long ago what some of my op-
> tions were in life. For me it's really simple. As
> much as I stray, I know that my ultimate goal is
> simply to have Him guide me on the right path
> for His name's sake. How do we know if it is the
> Lord speaking or someone else? The only
> answer I know is to become very familiar with His
> voice by spending time alone with Him.

I found *two things that have helped me get to know God again.* If you want to get to know God better, these tools may be helpful to you, too.

First, I started using a little devotional book by Dick Purnell called *Knowing God by His Names.*[1] It only takes about twenty minutes to do the suggested reading and devotional work, and it helped me get to know God and who He really is. By learning about the many names used for God throughout the Bible, you will also learn about His character and qualities.

Second, it is common knowledge that as Christians, we need to read the Bible. A variety of daily reading programs and many suggestions on how to accomplish them are available. If you are currently involved in a reading program that you are happy with, stay with it. I tried one of those programs where you read some of the Old Testament, New Testament, Psalms and Proverbs each day. I found that after I had completed the reading, I had no idea what I had just read.

If you have had similar struggles in daily reading, I suggest you try *The Narrated Bible* (also called *The Daily Bible* in paperback). This particular Bible is divided into daily reading sections—like many other programs—but the Scriptures are included, in chronological order. This makes your understanding of the events taking place much better.

In addition, there is "narration" along with the text. You may find that in one sitting you are reading from Samuel, Chronicles and Psalms but the verses you will read are arranged in the actual order the events took place. The commentary in with the text helps you understand the history, customs and significance of that portion of Scripture.

I learned many new things as I read through the Old Testament passages. For example, I remembered reading that Adam lived to be 930 years old. I knew the story of Noah well. But, until I read *The Narrated Bible*, I never realized that Adam lived long enough to tell the story of creation personally to every generation almost up to Noah's time. That was not earthshattering news, but it helped me to put the history into place.

Then I read about Aaron. I knew from Sunday school about Aaron and the golden calf. I knew that Aaron had helped the entire nation of Israel turn away from God while Moses was up on the mountain. I also knew a separate story about the tabernacle and I knew God had appointed Aaron to be the high priest. Until I read *The Narrated Bible,* I never connected the two stories. Through its reading I realized that if God could forgive Aaron for something as awful as leading the entire nation of Israel astray, and make him the spiritual leader of the country, certainly God could forgive us for our sins and use us for His glory.

If your daily relationship with God could use some strengthening, try these exceptional tools. I'm sure you will find they will help you get to really know God which is the first step toward hearing His voice and finding His direction for your life. Colossians 2:6 says: "And just as you trusted Christ to save you, trust him, too, for each day's problems; live in vital union with him" (TLB). It is that "vital union" that allows Him to help us with the decisions we need to make on a daily basis.

2. Pray Continually

Have you given thought to 1 Thessalonians 5:17? It says to "Pray constantly." We can't do that. Only a monk could truly "pray constantly." The rest of us live in the real world. We have to cook and drive car pool, go to work, and be involved in a variety of activities. How could God possibly expect us to be on our knees in prayer all the time?

I don't believe He intends that for us and I don't think I am in contradiction with Scripture. Romans 12:12 says to be "prayerful always" (TLB). As Christians our ultimate role model is Jesus Christ. When we study His life we see He was not on His knees in actual prayer "always." Prayer is really communion with our Father God and prayer can take many forms. It can be casually spoken while driving down the freeway; it can be formally done on our knees at the altar; it can be written; it can even be unspoken—a matter of attitude.

To pray continually is a combination of all of those. As we look at Christ's life, we see that, although He was not on His knees in formal prayer all the time, He did have an attitude of involving His heavenly Father in all He did, both big things and little things.

Like Christ, we need to have an attitude of wanting God in every part of our lives. When we are in that type of daily communion with Him, we can easily hear His response to our needs. I remember one day when my husband bought a car. It was a classic old Jaguar just like he had always wanted. It wasn't in very good shape and it needed a lot of attention. Because of our finances this car had to be the one Chuck drove every day. That meant he had to work on it every night so it would be okay to drive the next day. I would come home from work, fix dinner and call Chuck to come in from the garage and eat. He would come in, wash up, and eat in a hurry so he could get back out to his car. After a few days of his constant work on the Jaguar, I got very jealous of that stupid car.

One night after he had gone back out to the garage, I followed Christ's example in Matthew 14:23. I went up to the mountaintop to pray alone. I went upstairs into the bathroom, closed the door and sat on the toilet. I prayed, "Dear God, you have got to fix Chuck and make him see how wonderful I am."

Praying about a Jaguar doesn't seem highly spiritual and doing it while sitting on a toilet seems even less likely to create a spiritual experience, but there, God spoke to me. It was one of those times where His voice was so loud and clear I had to look around the room to see if anyone else was there.

He said to me, "Marita, that car provides Chuck with nothing but pleasure and when he spends time with you, he gets nagging and unhappiness. When he has spare time, who do you think he is going to spend it with?" I realized that the car was winning.

That was all God said to me, but the message was very clear. I changed my attitude about Chuck's hobby. I even learned to like the car, although I'm still afraid to drive it. I also have a plaque in my office now, a trophy I won as the second place navigator in an annual rally of the Jaguar Club of San Diego. Proof that my attitude has changed! As a result, Chuck spends more time with me, and when he does spend time on cars, I often help him.

For each of us, we need to get into the habit of coming to God with every detail of our lives, even the ones that are silly or embarrassing. If you feel God has spoken to you through the pages of this book in the development of a personal ministry, take your ideas to Him before launching out in a direction that might be good, but might not be His direction for your life.

3. Ask for Direction

Once you really know God and have that vital union with Him, and you have developed an attitude of having God involved in every detail of your life, you are ready to bring specific requests to Him. When we are looking for specific direction in our lives, we need to bring it to the Lord in prayer and ask. Ezekiel 36:37 tells us: "The Lord God says: I am ready to hear . . . and to grant them their requests. Let them but ask" (TLB).

When my color analysis business was booming and I had strayed from my close walk with the Lord, I didn't feel a need to call on Him. But after He closed that door and I was locked out in the hallway, I had to come crawling back on my hands and knees to Him. Our relationship was eventually restored and I again had that vital union with God. I pleaded with Him and I asked for His direction for my life. As I was able to let go of the door He had closed on my color analysis business, I was able to move on down the hallway, and God opened the next door.

I clearly remember how it happened. I was driving the familiar road from San Bernardino, where my parents lived and where their office was, to San Diego, where I live. It was a long empty road. A nice freeway with very little traffic. As I often did, I made the trip in prayer. I talked out loud to God and told Him my feelings, frustrations and needs. About halfway home I began asking God for specific direction for my life. At this point, about two years after my color analysis business had died, I had been maintaining several different jobs to earn a living but that's all I was doing—earning a living. I was ready for God to open the next door.

As I drove and prayed, I heard the voice of God as if He were sitting next to me. I knew what He said, but I couldn't articulate it to others until some time later. There in that car God gave me the direction for my life and my future. He told me I would become a resource, like a clearing house, for Christian communicators. To my knowledge there was no such service in existence at that time, so I had a difficult time explaining to others what God had said to me. I didn't tell anyone at first, but His voice had been so loud and clear I couldn't ignore it. I had asked for direction for my life, and God had answered.

James 1:5 says:

> If you want to know what God wants you to do, ask him, and he will gladly tell you, for he is always ready to give a bountiful supply of wisdom to all who ask him (TLB).

If you are looking for direction for a personal ministry, or for some other part of your life, first have that intimate relationship with Him. Second, maintain a continual attitude of prayer, inviting God to be a part of every aspect of your life. Verses 7 and 8 of Psalm 32 tell us that God will lead us in the best pathway for our lives. So, third, ask Him for direction—and then wait for His answer.

4. Wait for the Lord

This is the hardest part. In our age of microwave ovens, drive-through restaurants and mobile phones, we have become accustomed to having everything we want, when we want it. Much to our distress, God doesn't work that way. We may ask for direction today and not get the answer for days, or weeks, or even years. If we look at the life of Moses, we can see God was definitely at work in his life and God truly guided every step Moses took. Yet Moses spent forty years in the desert caring for sheep while the nation of Israel was in need of a savior. Moses had to wait. The people of Israel had to wait, and we too, must wait.

I spent nearly three years waiting for God to answer my prayer for direction. I call that time in my life the hallway. I was between doors that were both closed. I didn't just sit and collect unemployment, though. Like Moses, I worked, but I knew the work I was doing wasn't God's ultimate plan for my life. I had odd jobs, some of which ultimately added to God's direction for my life and others that were just a holding place for me, the hallway.

Waiting isn't fun, but it is an important learning time for us. As Psalm 27:14 says: "Don't be impatient. Wait for the Lord . . . Yes, wait and He will help you" (TLB).

While you are waiting keep in daily contact with the Lord so you can hear His voice. I have found God doesn't talk to us when we are so distracted by life's daily events that we can't hear Him. God talks to me when I am focused on Him and the situation at hand, when I am quiet and alone. I hear His voice when I am driving alone, when I am at the beach, or alone in the bathroom. I have talked with others who have felt God's direct input in their lives, and they all agree He only talks to them when they slow down enough to hear His voice. Moses went to the mountaintop to hear from God. Jesus went up to the mountains by Himself to spend time with His Father. We must wait alone for God's answer.

Weigh Your Thoughts

I have seen many good people head off in what proved to be a wrong direction while claiming it to be what God had told them to do. How can someone be so sure of God's direction and have it end in failure? Was God wrong? Did He change His mind?

I don't think so. One of the reasons we read Scripture is so that we can see God work in the lives of the biblical characters and use that as an example for His work in our own lives. God didn't make mistakes, nor did He change His mind. It has been my experience that we often want something so badly we pray for God's guidance and then hear the answer from our own subconscious.

I remember Betty. She came to one of our CLASS seminars and then she came to the Advanced CLASS. After the third day of Advanced CLASS she announced to the staff that she now knew what God wanted her to do with her life. We often hear similar comments from those who attend as we have found that that is one of the ways God works through CLASS.

We waited anxiously to hear what the Lord had revealed to Betty. She said, "God has told me to go home and divorce my husband and go into full-time speaking."

Needless to say, we were shocked! Betty really believed that this was what God had told her to do.

Cases like Betty's have made me understand the need for us to weigh our thoughts. Even when we have a close, intimate relationship with God and are in daily communion with Him, sometimes when we ask for direction, the first thing that comes into our mind comes from our own wants and desires. That is why we need to weigh what we perceive to be answers to our prayers and be certain they balance with God's Word.

Betty truly thought her insights were from God. If she were to weigh her thoughts, though, she would see that the answer she believed to have received was in direct opposition to God's Word. He wouldn't ask us to do the opposite of His commandments, and divorce is certainly not something He would direct.

When we weigh our ideas with God's word, and find the idea in conflict with biblical teaching, we can be sure the idea is not from God and we need to keep waiting for His answer.

What if the answer you receive isn't something that is addressed in the Bible? Maybe you feel God has placed a clothing ministry on your heart. How can you tell if that is truly from God? There are no direct references against helping others' clothing needs, and there many verses that encourage such ministry. How can we tell if it is really God's plan for us? I believe this is where godly counsel comes in.

To help us weigh our ideas, we need the counsel of those whose lives bear the fruit of close contact with God to help us discern if the idea is from our own needs or if it is truly from God.

I had a friend who felt God had told her to put on an event somewhat like my Southern California Women's Retreat only on a bigger scale. She was sure this idea was from

God. Those of us around her questioned her motives; we didn't feel this idea was really from God but rather was fulfilling a personal need for glory and success. When we approached her with our concerns, she wasn't open to our input at all and continued to insist God had told her to do this. It is very difficult to disagree with someone who is sure they are on a mission from God. We were left with no choice but to throw up our hands and try to help make this event a success.

Three weeks before the event it became clear that it wasn't going to make it. She figured the costs and concluded she would lose less money if she canceled the event than she would if she went ahead with it. At least fifty thousand dollars was lost because she hadn't weighed her thoughts and she refused wise counsel.

In her heart my friend was sure her plans were from God. Isaiah 55:8 gives us warning: "My thoughts are not your thoughts, neither are your ways my ways, says the LORD." When you get an answer, be sure your ideas are really God's ideas.

When I felt God had spoken to me regarding my future, I didn't tell anyone at first. I continued to pray and ask for confirmation. As God continued to press the same answer on my heart, I decided to mention my idea to my parents. They were on their way home from their first trip to Australia and I drove a couple hours to pick them up at the Los Angeles airport. On the way home I told them what I felt God had suggested to me. My mother burst into tears.

Through the tears she told me that she and my dad had been praying I would be available to work full-time with them, but they didn't want to ask because they wanted it to be my idea. They didn't want me to feel pressured. And here I was laying out a plan that would involve my intimate involvement with the family ministry. God answered both our prayers and confirmed they were His plans all at the same time!

He has continued to open doors, doors that I would never have thought to try. It has been nearly five years since then. I have been amazed at the plan God has for me. What started out as just me booking a few speaking engagements for those who had been through our CLASS seminar has expanded to my helping my mother get on TV and radio programs to let people know about her books. Today my staff of four and I work with churches from all over the country who call us looking for speakers for all kinds of events. We help speakers manage their calendars and organize their speaking schedules. We now work with from ten to fifteen publishers at a time and we get their authors on TV and radio programs all over the country. I still teach our CLASS seminars with my mother and the rest of our teaching staff. I speak myself at many different women's events throughout the country, and I've written a few books.

In the last year my parents have moved near me in the San Diego area and they have moved the ministry offices, both theirs and mine into a lovely new facility.

When God gave me the vision to be a resource for Christian communicators, I had no idea what He had in mind, but it is exciting to know that where I am is where God wants me!

Thank Him

Once we have received our answers and confirmed they are from Him, we must be sure to thank Him. Philippians 4:6 sums up the whole process by saying:

> Don't worry about anything; instead, pray about everything; tell God your needs and don't forget to thank him for his answers (TLB).

God will give you direction for your life. If you are one of His sheep, you'll be able to hear His voice. Stay in close daily communion with Him, ask for His direction, and wait for His answers. When you get an answer, weigh it to be sure it is truly from God and then thank Him for it.

As you have read the different ways you can Give Back, God may have spoken to you and placed a ministry idea on your heart. Let me again caution you, before you embark on a mission, be sure the road you take is the one God wants for you.

When you are sure of your direction, get started. You are on the road toward Giving Back!

Would You Like to Know God Personally?

The following four principles will help you discover how to know God personally and experience the abundant life He promised.

1 GOD **LOVES** YOU AND CREATED YOU TO KNOW HIM PERSONALLY.

(References contained in these pages should be read in context from the Bible whenever possible.)

God's Love

"For God so loved the world, that He gave His only begotten Son, that whoever believes in Him should not perish, but have eternal life" (John 3:16).

God's Plan

"Now this is eternal life: that they may know you, the only true God, and Jesus Christ, whom you have sent" (John 17:3, NIV).

What prevents us from knowing God personally?

2 MAN IS **SINFUL** AND **SEPARATED** FROM GOD, SO WE CANNOT KNOW HIM PERSONALLY OR EXPERIENCE HIS LOVE.

Man Is Sinful

"For all have sinned and fall short of the glory of God" (Romans 3:23).

Man was created to have fellowship with God; but, because of his stubborn self-will, he chose to go his own independent way, and fellowship with God was broken. This self-will, characterized by an attitude of active rebellion or passive indifference, is evidence of what the Bible calls sin.

Man Is Separated

"For the wages of sin is death" (spiritual separation from God) (Romans 6:23).

This diagram illustrates that God is holy and man is sinful. A great gulf separates the two. The arrows illustrate that man is continually trying to reach God and establish a personal relationship with Him through his own efforts, such as a good life, philosophy or religion.

The third principle explains the only way to bridge this gulf . . .

3 JESUS CHRIST IS GOD'S ONLY PROVISION FOR MAN'S SIN. THROUGH HIM ALONE WE CAN KNOW GOD PERSONALLY AND EXPERIENCE HIS LOVE.

He Died in Our Place

"But God demonstrates His own love toward us, in that while we were yet sinners, Christ died for us" (Romans 5:8).

He Rose From the Dead

"Christ died for our sins . . . He was buried . . . He was raised on the third day, according to the Scriptures . . . He appeared to Peter, then to the twelve. After that He appeared to more than five hundred" (1 Corinthians 15:3-6).

He Is the Only Way to God

"Jesus said to him, 'I am the way, and the truth, and the life; no one comes to the Father, but through Me' " (John 14:6).

This diagram illustrates that God has bridged the gulf which separates us from Him by sending His Son, Jesus Christ, to die on the cross in our place to pay the penalty for our sins.

It is not enough just to know these truths . . .

4 WE MUST INDIVIDUALLY RECEIVE JESUS CHRIST AS SAVIOR AND LORD; THEN WE CAN KNOW GOD PERSONALLY AND EXPERIENCE HIS LOVE.

We Must Receive Christ

"But as many as received Him, to them He gave the right to become children of God, even to those who believe in His name" (John 1:12).

We Receive Christ Through Faith

"For by grace you have been saved through faith; and that not of yourselves, it is the gift of God; not as a result of works, that no one should boast" (Ephesians 2:8,9).

When We Receive Christ, We Experience a New Birth. (Read John 3:1-8.)

We Receive Christ by Personal Invitation

(Christ is speaking): "Behold, I stand at the door and knock; if anyone hears My voice and opens the door, I will come in to him" (Revelation 3:20).

Receiving Christ involves turning to God from self (repentance) and trusting Christ to come into our lives to forgive our sins and to make us the kind of people He wants us to be. Just to agree intellectually that Jesus Christ is the Son of God and that He died on the cross for our sins is not enough. Nor is it enough to have an emotional experience. We receive Jesus Christ by faith, as an act of the will.

These two circles represent two kinds of lives:

SELF-DIRECTED LIFE
S – Self is on the throne
† – Christ is outside the life
• – Interests are directed by self, often resulting in discord and frustration

CHRIST-DIRECTED LIFE
† – Christ is in the life and on the throne
S – Self is yielding to Christ
• – Interests are directed by Christ, resulting

The following explains how you can invite Jesus Christ into your life:

YOU CAN RECEIVE CHRIST RIGHT NOW BY FAITH THROUGH PRAYER

(Prayer is talking with God)

God knows your heart and is not so concerned with your words as He is with the attitude of your heart. The following is a suggested prayer:

"Lord Jesus, I want to know You personally. Thank You for dying on the cross for my sins. I open the door of my life and receive You as my Savior and Lord. Thank You for forgiving my sins and giving me eternal life. Take control of the throne of my life. Make me the kind of person You want me to be."

Does this prayer express the desire of your heart?

If it does, pray this prayer right now, and Christ will come into your life, as He promised.

How to Know That Christ Is in Your Life

Did you receive Christ into your life? According to His promise in Revelation 3:20, where is Christ right now in relation to you? Christ said that He would come into your life and be your friend so you can know Him personally. Would He mislead you? On what authority do you know that God has answered your prayer? (The trustworthiness of God Himself and His Word.)

The Bible Promises Eternal Life to All Who Receive Christ

"And the witness is this, that God has given us eternal life, and this life is in His Son. He who has the Son has the life; he who does not have the Son of God does not have the life. These things I have written to you who believe in the name of the Son of God, in order that you may know that you have eternal life" (1 John 5:11-13).

Thank God often that Christ is in your life and that He will never leave you (Hebrews 13:5). You can know on the basis of His promise that Christ lives in you and that you have eternal life, from the very moment you invite Him in. He will not deceive you.

An important reminder . . .

DO NOT DEPEND ON FEELINGS

The promise of God's Word, the Bible — not our feelings — is our authority. The Christian lives by faith (trust) in the trustworthiness of God Himself and His Word. This train diagram illustrates the relationship between fact (God and His Word), faith (our trust in God and His Word), and feeling (the result of our faith and obedience) (John 14:21).

The train will run with or without the caboose. However, it would be useless to attempt to pull the train by the caboose. In the same way, we, as Christians, do not depend on feelings or emotions, but we place our faith (trust) in the trustworthiness of God and the promises of His Word.

Fellowship in a Good Church

God's Word admonishes us not to forsake "the assembling of ourselves together" (Hebrews 10:25). Several logs burn brightly together, but put one aside on the cold hearth and the fire goes out. So it is with your relationship with other Christians. If you do not belong to a church, do not wait to be invited. Take the initiative; call the pastor of a nearby church where Christ is honored and His Word is preached. Start this week, and make plans to attend regularly.

Suggestions for Christian Growth

Spiritual growth results from trusting Jesus Christ. "The righteous man shall live by faith" (Galatians 3:11). A life of faith will enable you to trust God increasingly with every detail of your life.

Reference Notes

Introduction
1. Oswald Chambers, *My Utmost for His Highest* (New York: Dodd, Mead & Co., 1935; renewed by Oswald Chambers Publications, Ltd., 1963), n.p.

Chapter 1 What Is "Giving Back"?
1. Acts 20:35.
2. Oswald Chambers, *My Utmost for His Highest* (New York: Dodd, Mead & Co., 1935; renewed by Oswald Chambers Publications, Ltd., 1963), n.p.

Chapter 12 Listening
1. A. W. Tozer, *Listening: A Christian's Guide* (n.p., n.d.), p. 112.

Chapter 13 Complete Confidence Through the Vital Union
1. Dick Purnell, *Knowing God by His Names, A 31-Day Experiment* (San Bernardino, CA: Here's Life Publishers, 1987).

Life-Changing Reading

Quantity   Total

_____ **Your Mighty Fortress** by Sherwood Eliot Wirt. In this $_____
thoughtful, insightful book, Sherwood Wirt shares
how you can cultivate an inner life with Christ leading
to joy, contentment and intimacy. $7.99

_____ **Don't Just Stand There, Pray Something** by $_____
Ronald Dunn. An inspiring look at how you can pray
with greater purpose and power — for your own needs
as well as the needs of others. $7.99

_____ **Make the Tough Times Count** by Florence Littauer. $_____
With her trademark poignancy and humor, one of
America's most inspirational speakers shares how
you can learn to rise above adversities. $8.99

_____ **When Your Dreams Die** by Marilyn Willett Heavilin. $_____
If you or someone you know has experienced tragedy
or disappointment, this noted expert on grief recovery
provides gentle comfort and practical guidance. $7.99

**Your Christian bookseller should have these products in stock.
Please check with him before using this "Shop by Mail" form.**

Indicate product(s) desired above. Fill out below.
Send to:

HERE'S LIFE PUBLISHERS, INC.
P. O. Box 1576
San Bernardino, CA 92402-1576

NAME_____

ADDRESS_____

CITY_____

STATE_____ZIP_____

❏ Payment included
    (check or money order only)
❏ Visa   ❏ Mastercard #_____

Expiration Date_____Signature _____

**FOR FASTER SERVICE
CALL TOLL FREE: 1-800-950-4457**

ORDER TOTAL $_____

**SHIPPING and
HANDLING** $_____
($1.50 for one book,
$0.50 for each additional.
Do not exceed $4.00.)

**APPLICABLE
SALES TAX** $_____
(CA 6.75%)

TOTAL DUE $_____
PAYABLE IN U.S. FUNDS.
(No cash orders accepted.)

GB 324-3